NARCISSISM

How to Stop Narcissistic Abuse,
Heal Your Relationships, and
Transform Your Life

JUDY DYER

NARCISSISM: How to Stop Narcissistic Abuse, Heal
Your Relationships, and Transform Your Life
by Judy Dyer

© Copyright 2019 by Judy Dyer

All Rights Reserved.

Disclaimer: This book is designed to provide accurate and author-itative information in regard to the subject matter covered. By its sale, neither the publisher nor the author is engaged in rendering psychological or other professional services. If expert assistance or counseling is needed, the services of a competent professional should be sought.

ISBN-10: 1705410561
ISBN-13: 978-1705410561

ALSO BY JUDY DYER

*Empath: A Complete Guide for Developing Your Gift
and Finding Your Sense of Self*

*The Highly Sensitive: How to Stop Emotional Overload,
Relieve Anxiety, and Eliminate Negative Energy*

*The Empowered Empath: A Simple Guide on Setting
Boundaries, Controlling Your Emotions, and Making Life Easier*

*Narcissist: A Complete Guide for Dealing with Narcissism
and Creating the Life You Want*

Empaths and Narcissists: 2 in 1 Bundle

Empath and The Highly Sensitive: 2 in 1 Bundle

*Borderline Personality Disorder: A Complete BPD Guide for
Managing Your Emotions and Improving Your Relationships*

CONTENTS

INTRODUCTION

"I think my ex is a narcissist."

"My father is so narcissistic."

"I think my boss has Narcissistic Personality Disorder."

Narcissism is a popular topic these days. Everyone wants to know how to spot a narcissist, how to deal with them, and whether they can "cure" their narcissist partner, friend, or relative.

On the whole, this is a good thing. Narcissistic individuals cause a lot of damage. It's great that people are talking about this issue openly. Narcissists are everywhere in society, and learning how to protect yourself against them is a smart move.

The downside is that there's far too much information out there. If you're just starting to get to grips with the concept of narcissism, where should you start? What sources can you trust? Exactly how many books, articles, and blog posts do you need to read before you really understand the problem?

If you think you're dealing with a narcissist, you probably have a lot of questions. This book will answer them. By the time you've finished reading, you'll have all the tools you need to defend yourself against narcissistic people.

We'll look at what narcissism is, how to identify it, and how to deal with narcissists of all shapes and sizes. Whether the narcissist in your life is a partner, friend, family member, boss, or colleague, you have the power to limit the fallout and reclaim your life.

Narcissistic behavior is confusing, and even terrifying at times, but it's also strangely predictable. Once you understand the psychology of a narcissist, you'll start to see the same old patterns recurring again and again. You'll be able to anticipate what they'll say and do next, which lets you regain control over the situation.

There's no need to live in fear of narcissists. If you're willing to follow the practical tips in this book, your life will quickly become much easier. Your relationships will improve, and you'll no longer be at the mercy of manipulative individuals.

Turn the page, and let's get started.

JOIN OUR SUPPORT GROUP

In order to maximize the value you receive from this book, I highly encourage you to join our tight-knit community on Facebook. Here you will be able to connect and share strategies with others dealing with narcissists in order to continue your growth.

Taking this journey alone is not recommended, and this can be an excellent support network for you.

It would be great to connect with you there,

Judy Dyer

To Join, Visit: www.pristinepublish.com/empathgroup

Or Scan the QR Code on Your Phone:

DOWNLOAD THE AUDIO VERSION OF THIS BOOK FREE

If you love listening to audiobooks on-the-go or would enjoy a narration as you read along, I have great news for you. You can download the audiobook version of Narcissism for FREE (Regularly $14.95) just by signing up for a FREE 30-day audible trial!

Visit: www.pristinepublish.com/audiobooks

Or Scan the QR Code on Your Phone:

YOUR FREE GIFT - HEYOKA EMPATH

A lot of empaths feel trapped, as if they've hit a glass ceiling they can't penetrate. They know there's another level to their gift, but they can't seem to figure out what it is. They've read dozens of books, been to counselling, and confided in other experienced empaths, but that glass ceiling remains. They feel alone, and alienated from the rest of the world because they know they've got so much more to give, but can't access it. Does this sound like you?

The inability to connect to your true and authentic self is a tragedy. Being robbed of the joy of embracing the full extent of your humanity is a terrible misfortune. The driving force of human nature is to live according to one's own sense of self, values, and emotions. Since the beginning of time, philosophers, writers, and scholars have argued that authenticity is one of the most important elements of an individual's well-being.

When there's a disconnect between a person's inner being and their expressions, it can be psychologically damaging. Heyokas are the most powerful type of empaths, and many of them are not fully aware of who they are. While other empaths experience feelings of overwhelm and exhaustion from absorbing others' energy and emotions, heyoka empaths experience an additional aspect of exhaustion in that they are fighting a constant battle with their inability to be completely authentic.

The good news is that the only thing stopping you from becoming your authentic self is a lack of knowledge. You need to know exactly who you are so you can tap into the resources that have been lying dormant within you. In this bonus e-book, you'll gain in-depth information about the seven signs that you're a heyoka empath, and why certain related abilities are such powerful traits. You'll find many of the answers to the questions you've been searching for your entire life such as:

- Why you feel uncomfortable when you're around certain people
- How you always seem to find yourself on the right path even though your decisions are not based on logic or rationale
- The reason you get so offended when you find out others have lied to you
- Why you analyze everything in such detail
- The reason why humor is such an important part of your life
- Why you refuse to follow the crowd, regardless of the consequences
- The reason why strangers and animals are drawn to you

There are three main components to authenticity: understanding who you are, expressing who you are, and letting the world experience who you are. Your first step on this journey is to know who you are, and with these seven signs that you're a heyoka empath, you'll find out. I've included snippets about the first three signs in this description to give you full confidence that you're on the right track:

Sign 1: You Feel and Understand Energy

Heyoka empaths possess a natural ability to tap into energy. They can walk into a room and immediately discern the atmosphere. When an individual walks past them, they can literally see into their soul because they can sense the aura that person is carrying. But empaths also understand their own energy, and they allow it to guide them. You will often hear this ability referred to as "the sixth sense." The general consensus is that only a few people have this gift. But the reality is that everyone was born with the ability to feel energy; it's just been demonized and turned into something spooky, when in actual fact, it's the most natural state to operate in.

Sign 2: You are Led by Your Intuition

Do you find that you just know things? You don't spend hours, days, and weeks agonizing over decisions, you can just feel that something is the right thing to do, and you go ahead and do it. That's because you're led by your intuition and you're connected to the deepest part of yourself. You know your soul, you listen to it, and you trust it. People like Oprah Winfrey, Steve Jobs and Richard Branson followed their intuition steadfastly and it led them to become some of the most successful people in the history of the world.

Living from within is the way we were created to be, and those who trust this ability will find their footing in life a lot more quickly than others. Think of it as a GPS system: when it's been programmed properly, it will always take you to your destination via the fastest route.

Sign 3: You Believe in Complete Honesty

In general, empaths don't like being around negative energy, and there's nothing that can shift a positive frequency faster than dishonesty. Anything that isn't the truth is a lie, even the tiny ones that we excuse away as "white lies." And as soon as they're released from someone's mouth, so is negative energy. Living an authentic life requires complete honesty at all times, and although the truth may hurt, it's better than not being able to trust someone. Heyoka empaths get very uncomfortable in the presence of liars. They are fully aware that the vibrations of the person don't match the words they are saying. Have you ever experienced a brain freeze mid-conversation? All of a sudden you just couldn't think straight, you couldn't articulate yourself properly, and things just got really awkward? That's because your empath antenna picked up on a lie.

Heyoka Empath: 7 Signs You're A Heyoka Empath & Why It's So Powerful is a revolutionary tool that will help you transition from uncertainty to complete confidence in who you are. In this easy-to-read guide, I will walk you through exactly what makes you a heyoka empath. I've done the research for you, so no more spending hours, days, weeks, and even years searching for answers, because everything you need is right here in this book.

You have a deep need to share yourself with the world, but you've been too afraid because you knew something was missing. The information within the pages of this book is the missing piece in the jigsaw puzzle of your life. There's no turning back now!

Get *Heyoka Empath* for Free by Visiting

www.pristinepublish.com/empathbonus

Or Scan the QR Code on Your Phone:

CHAPTER 1:

WHAT EXACTLY DOES IT MEAN TO BE A NARCISSIST?

B efore we dive into practical strategies, we need to get clear on what "narcissism" and "narcissistic personality disorder (NPD)" mean.

NARCISSISM

A narcissistic person puts their own needs and wishes before those of other people. They believe themselves to be better and more interesting than everyone else, and their behavior reflects their attitude.[1] They suck up all the air in the room, feel entitled to special treatment, and thrive on attention.

You can think of narcissism as a spectrum. Most of us are a little bit narcissistic. It's normal to occasionally brag about your accomplishments, fish for compliments, or to overestimate your abilities.

The trouble starts when your narcissism hurts others. People high in narcissism often alienate their coworkers, hurt their friends, and leave their partners confused and wounded by their behaviors.

It's helpful to divide narcissistic behavior into three categories:[2]

Ordinary ("Normal") Narcissism: Occasional displays of selfishness, insensitivity, and self-importance are annoying, but they are part of what makes us human. If you catch yourself feeling slightly grandiose from time to time, or dominating a conversation, don't panic. It doesn't mean you're a narcissist. No one is a saint, after all.

Narcissistic Personality Type: Further along the narcissist spectrum are those with a narcissistic personality. These people are frequently vain, attention-seeking, and crave never-ending validation. However, although they are difficult to live or work with, psychologists still consider them to be within the realms of "normal." It's an unfortunate fact of life that some people just have unpleasant personalities.

Pathological Narcissism, or Narcissistic Personality Disorder (NPD): At the far end of the narcissism scale, we have people with NPD. Unlike those with a narcissistic personality type, people with NPD have a diagnosable disorder that negatively impacts their lives and hurts those around them. Only medical professionals with appropriate training are qualified to identify someone with NPD, but the symptoms are usually obvious.

WHAT IS A PERSONALITY DISORDER?

Personality disorders consist of rigid, destructive ways of thinking and behaving that are usually present from adolescence. Because these patterns are so engrained by early adulthood, personality disorders are hard to treat.

People with NPD are obsessed with gaining approval, admiration, and social status. They are self-absorbed to the point where normal relationships become impossible. They lack empathy, meaning they don't understand how their actions affect others.

Extreme narcissists are rare. Around 0.5-1% of the population meet the criteria for NPD, as defined in the Diagnostic and Statistical Manual of Mental Disorders. One half to three-quarters are male.[3]

According to the American Psychiatric Association, NPD entails "a pervasive pattern of grandiosity (in fantasy or behavior), a constant need for admiration, and a lack of empathy...as indicated by the presence of at least 5 of the following 9 criteria:"[4]

- A grandiose sense of self-importance
- Preoccupation with fantasies of unlimited success, power, brilliance, beauty, or ideal love
- A belief that he or she is special and unique and can only be understood by, or associate with, other special or high-status people or institutions
- A need for excessive admiration
- A sense of entitlement
- Interpersonally exploitative behavior

- A lack of empathy
- Envy of others or a belief that others are envious of him or her
- A demonstration of arrogant or haughty behaviors or attitudes

It's common for people with NPD to abuse alcohol or illegal substances, and they may experience other mental health problems, such as depression and anxiety.

In this book, the term "narcissist" is used to describe someone with NPD. However, the strategies you'll learn will also help you deal with anyone who regularly shows narcissistic behaviors, whether or not they meet the formal diagnostic criteria listed above.

The Two Types Of Pathological Narcissists

Most psychologists divide narcissists into two subgroups, each with their own set of distinctive characteristics:[5]

Grandiose Narcissists: These people fit the classic narcissist stereotype. They like to brag about their achievements to anyone who will listen. They love to be around other people, and they are normally upbeat. They want to seize power and aren't subtle about it. They love impressing others.

Although their default mood is positive, grandiose narcissists can become depressed when their grand schemes and plans don't work out. They have an unrealistic view of their own abilities. However, they can still succeed in life and work, partly because their high levels of confidence can trick others into thinking they are more competent than they really are.

Vulnerable Narcissists: These narcissists are more introverted and reclusive. At the same time, they believe they are entitled to pity, attention, and special accommodations. For example, a depressed vulnerable narcissist won't consider how their moodiness and bleak outlook affects others. They may expect friends or family to care for them around the clock or support them financially.

Vulnerable narcissists may be capable of helping themselves, but their egos often get in the way before they can make any real progress. For instance, they might be able to get a new job if they are unemployed but refuse to accept one unless they are guaranteed a high-status position. They are angrier, more envious, and more hostile than grandiose narcissists.

Although grandiose and vulnerable narcissists appear quite different, they share several things in common. Both are disagreeable, self-centered, happy to exploit other people, and believe they are entitled to special treatment. Both types lack the ability to enjoy balanced relationships with other people, and both will always value their own needs and goals above all else.

ARE THERE OTHER TYPES OF NARCISSISM?

If you Google "different types of narcissism" or similar terms, you'll find lots of articles that describe other forms of narcissism.

For example, you may stumble across these labels:

Somatic narcissist: A narcissist who is obsessed with their appearance. They might post lots of photos on their social media profiles, spend an excessive amount of time at the gym, and fish for compliments every chance they get. Somatic narcissists fear aging because youth and beauty are so important to them. They might have a lot of cosmetic surgery.

Cerebral narcissist: "Cerebral narcissism" is a label used to describe someone who is convinced that they are far more intelligent and knowledgeable than those around them. They enjoy correcting people but refuse to be corrected themselves.

Sometimes, these individuals are actually smart, but many cerebral narcissists actually have average IQs. It isn't their intellectual capacity that sets them apart, but their arrogant attitude and belief in their own superiority.

Inverted narcissist: An "inverted narcissist" is someone who feels the need to be in a relationship with a narcissist. They aren't narcissistic in their own right, but they might show unhealthy traits that come to the foreground only when they are committed to a true narcissist.[6]

It's best to think of an inverted narcissist as someone who is suffering from a dependent disorder. Just like someone who abuses alcohol or drugs to the point of addiction, an inverted narcissist struggles to cope without a narcissist by their side. They look to the narcissist for direction, and this leaves them vulnerable to abuse.

For the sake of simplicity, we're going to talk about grandiose and vulnerable narcissists in this book. The "grandiose versus vulnerable" distinction is widely accepted by psychologists and psychiatrists, whereas the other subtypes are more controversial.

However, it's still important to be aware of the other terms listed above because you might see them used in online discussion groups or articles.

What Causes NPD?

Psychologists aren't sure what causes NPD, but it's probably a combination of genetics and upbringing. Experts have identified a few childhood risk factors that make it more likely someone will develop the disorder. These include trauma, being raised by parents who hold unrealistic expectations for their children, and childhood abuse.[7]

Note that most people with these childhood risk factors don't develop NPD, and it's impossible to pin down a single cause in most cases.

A rough childhood never excuses someone's behavior. If someone acts in an abusive or destructive manner as an adult, they need to be held accountable for their actions. You may feel sorry for someone with NPD, but this doesn't mean you have any kind of obligation to tolerate or forgive them.

Do Narcissists Secretly Have Low Self-Esteem?

One popular belief about narcissists is that their behaviors compensate for a lack of self-esteem. Some people believe that, deep down, narcissists are self-hating. According to this theory, narcissistic behaviors are a kind of protective shield. This is sometimes known as the "mask theory."

But is there actually a relationship between narcissism and low self-esteem? It's complicated. Psychologists have been trying to understand this link for decades. Some studies suggest that they do indeed use a persona to hide feelings of low self-worth, but recent research indicates that people diagnosed with NPD actually have normal levels of self-esteem.[8]

Some psychologists believe that a narcissist's underlying problem isn't low self-esteem; the real issue is that they are unusually bad at regulating their self-image.[9] This causes them to lash out whenever their ego is threatened.

To understand this theory, consider how "normal" people deal with setbacks. Most people doubt themselves from time to time. For example, it's normal for your self-esteem to take a knock when you fail an exam or get rejected by a love interest. Fortunately, we can usually pick ourselves back up, remind ourselves of our strengths, and move on. People with NPD often lack this skill. They are more affected by the normal ups and downs of everyday life.

In short, it appears that narcissists don't necessarily have low self-esteem, but their egos are more fragile than the average individual. They are also more likely to use unhealthy coping mechanisms, such as angry outbursts, to combat feelings of low self-esteem whenever their sense of superiority is challenged.[10]

If you're interested in this topic, there are dozens of academic papers published in psychology journals online. But, for our purposes, it's enough to say that the relationship between narcissism and self-esteem isn't straightforward. The mask theory, despite what you may have read online, isn't infallible. What's more, each narcissist is slightly different in how they cope with life's challenges.

CAN NPD BE TREATED?

In theory, yes. Talking therapy can help someone with NPD learn healthier ways of behaving around other people. Medication and therapy can help with other mental health problems someone with NPD might be experiencing, such as depression or substance abuse.

In practice, it's a bit more complicated than that. Narcissists don't usually think there's anything wrong with them, so most don't start therapy.

It's not that narcissists lack self-awareness. In fact, they usually acknowledge that they are narcissists. Some go a step further and embrace their dysfunctional personalities. Some point out that their traits have helped them get great jobs or high-status positions. Others openly admire people who succeed by "beating" others.

Research has shown that narcissistic people genuinely believe themselves to be superior to everyone else, but they are also aware that they have traits that others dislike, such as arrogance and impulsivity. They also recognize that those around them see them as narcissistic.[11]

Although most narcissists don't want to change, some psychologists believe that most can, and will, learn new relationship skills if they realize it will improve their lives.

According to psychotherapist and psychologist Craig Malkin,[12] narcissists tend to feel insecure in their relationships, and their dysfunctional behaviors give them an illusion of safety. He advises that by learning to trust their own emotions and connect with people on a meaningful level, some people with NPD can "recover."

However, even when they do want to change, there's another hurdle to overcome. Narcissists assume they are smarter than the person treating them. As you can imagine, this makes the treatment process long and difficult.

AIM TO MANAGE (NOT TREAT) NARCISSISTS AROUND YOU

This book focuses on coping strategies you can use in your day-to-day life rather than interventions for people with NPD. Don't fall into the trap of spending your precious energy trying to change the unchangeable. You'll save yourself a lot of heartache if you can accept a narcissist for who they are. Don't try to force them into therapy. Put yourself first.

In the next chapter, we'll look at how to identify the narcissists in your life.

SUMMARY

- Narcissistic people are highly self-absorbed, lack empathy, and feel entitled to special treatment.
- We are all narcissistic to some degree because narcissism is a trait that occurs on a spectrum.
- People who are very narcissistic may have a narcissistic personality type, or Narcissistic Personality Disorder (NPD) in extreme cases.
- NPD has a specific set of diagnostic criteria, as laid out in the DSM-V.
- It's likely that NPD has multiple causes.
- Most psychologists agree that people with NPD are either grandiose or vulnerable narcissists.
- Vulnerable narcissists are harder to spot than the grandiose type, but both have key similarities in common.
- NPD is hard to treat.

CHAPTER 2:

SPOTTING NARCISSISTS IN YOUR EVERYDAY LIFE

D o you suspect that someone you know is a narcissist? In this chapter, we'll move beyond criteria and diagnostic labels and look at narcissism in the real world.

RED FLAGS YOU CAN'T AFFORD TO IGNORE

If you know what to look for, you can spot a narcissist pretty quickly. Sometimes, you'll know within a few minutes that the person in front of you is toxic.

Here are some key signs:

1. *They are unusually charming.*

   We all appreciate good manners, but if someone seems determined to charm you, watch out. Narcissists are masters at making people feel special. A narcissist will flatter you. They may tell you how interesting, beautiful, or "amazing" you are. In reality, they don't care about you as a person. Instead, they are satisfying their own ego by winning your admiration.

The average narcissist can't and won't build steady, healthy relationships based on good communication and honesty. They might appear very interested in you one day, then seem indifferent the next. Their primary goal is to get and hold your attention.

2. *They like to dominate the conversation.*
    Someone who always monopolizes a conversation might be a narcissist. If they talk about their opinions, hobbies, and experiences without drawing breath, tread carefully.

    Bear in mind that some people talk too much when they are nervous, so this behavior doesn't automatically mean someone is a narcissist. However, it's a common sign.

3. *They don't respect your boundaries.*
    Narcissists overstep boundaries in subtle and not so subtle ways, from inappropriate touching to overly personal questions. Narcissists hate to be told "No" because they believe the world should cater to their demands.

    They may tell you far too much about their health, relationships, or personal problems. This tactic lures you into a false sense of security, makes you trust them, and therefore encourages you to share your own secrets. This gives a narcissist ammunition to use against you later.

4. *They like to give unsolicited advice.*

   Because they believe themselves to be much smarter than they really are, a narcissist will be quick to offer their advice, even when you didn't ask for it. If you dare tell them that their input is neither wanted nor necessary, they become angry. They cannot understand why you wouldn't want their opinion. After all, from their point of view, they are the cleverest person in the room.

5. *They just can't seem to wait for anything.*

   Most people find it annoying to wait around for something, but narcissists find it unbearable. They try to jump queues and manipulate others into giving them preferential treatment. They don't seem to understand that the world doesn't run according to their schedule.

6. *They stick to their opinions like glue.*

   Inflexible thinking is a hallmark of a narcissist. They don't believe that anything anyone else has to say can possibly be more insightful than their own thoughts, so why should they change their opinion?

   Ask a narcissist to justify or explain their position, and you might be met with contempt or even rage. They don't feel accountable to anyone but themselves. In their opinion, you should accept whatever they think and believe as gospel truth.

7. *They tell you stories about how they "triumphed" over other people.*

    In the world of a narcissist, people can be divided into two camps: "winners" and "losers." When they manage to take advantage of someone they perceive as weak (a "loser"), a narcissist will feel proud of themselves. If they think they've taken down a "winner," they'll be even more eager to tell you about it.

    If you're talking to someone who seems unusually proud that they exploited or manipulated someone else, you're probably in the company of a narcissist.

8. *They are rude to service staff and junior employees.*

    Everyone is entitled to respect, whatever their job or social position, but narcissists don't bother treating people well unless they can get something in return. For example, narcissists are often rude or indifferent to wait staff or people a few rungs down the employment ladder but will suddenly become charming in the presence of their boss.

9. *They happily describe themselves as a narcissist.*

    If someone describes themselves as a narcissist, you'd be wise to believe them. Remember, they don't think that there's anything wrong with their behavior. They might even think that you're jealous of them!

10. *They have unrealistic expectations.*

Remember the "grandiose fantasies" mentioned in the previous chapter? Narcissists tend to assume that their plans will work out, they will be extremely successful, and they will one day get the fame and fortune they deserve.

Even narcissists who have tried and failed many times will still cling to their fantasies. They will tell you what they could achieve, if only their circumstances were different. If you gently suggest that their plans aren't realistic, they'll get mad or say you have no idea what you're talking about.

11. *They are very interested in your social status.*

The further you are up the socioeconomic ladder, the more attractive you are to narcissists. They are shameless gold-diggers who will try to ingratiate themselves with popular, successful, rich people.

12. *They use unexpected gifts or favors to manipulate you.*

It's human nature to reciprocate. When someone gives you a compliment, does you a favor, or gives you a gift, your instinct is to give something back.

Narcissists exploit this impulse by granting you a favor or giving you a gift you didn't ask for, just so you'll be in their debt. This gives them a feeling of power over you.

13. *Nothing is ever their fault.*

    If a narcissist succeeds, they will take all the credit. If a narcissist fails, they'll usually find someone else to blame.

    However, a narcissist will sometimes play the victim card, lamenting their personal failures in an attempt to win sympathy. This is a favorite tactic of vulnerable narcissists.

    For instance, if their relationship breaks down, they will make a big show of claiming that the situation is entirely their fault. They may cry and reel off a list of reasons why they were the bad guy in the relationship. However, they don't really believe they are in the wrong. They just want others to reassure them that they aren't a terrible person, and hopefully get some compliments into the bargain.

14. *They break the rules.*

    Most of us bend the rules occasionally, but narcissists make a habit of it. For instance, narcissistic employees don't bother following workplace policies. Narcissistic spouses often cheat because they don't believe that the rules of a monogamous relationship really apply to them.

    Note that narcissists can have double standards. They think that anyone else who breaks the rules should be held to account, but they are always a special case.

15. *They have their own interpretation of reality.*
    A narcissist will go to any length to preserve their self-image as a special person. If they don't like the harsh reality of a situation, they'll just twist things around to suit themselves.

    For example, let's say a narcissist has been working for the same boss for a couple of years. They think that they are due a promotion and are angry because they believe their considerable talents have been overlooked.

In reality, the narcissist might be adequate at their job but not yet ready to take on a more senior role. At their annual review, their boss says that if they want to advance in the company, they will need to improve in several key areas.

Most people would feel disappointed in this situation, but a narcissist would find it intolerable. Rather than take an objective look at the problem, their first response would be to find someone else to blame, thus changing the narrative to suit themselves. For instance, they might decide that their boss is only acting out of spite or jealousy, and then spread rumors to this effect.

SPOTTING A NARCISSIST ONLINE

When browsing social media profiles, watch out for:

1. *Lots of shallow interactions with many people*
   Narcissists rarely have many meaningful friendships, but they like to look popular. From their perspective,

the more clicks and followers they have, the better. They prize quantity over quality.

2. *Unusually glamorous, staged, or unrealistic photos*
Narcissists want other people to feel jealous of their lifestyles. They'll post shots of expensive dinners, vacations, possessions, and exclusive social events. Don't be fooled; a narcissist will happily edit their posts to portray themselves in the best possible light.

3. *Attention-seeking content*
Grandiose narcissists will boast about their achievements on their social media profiles. Vulnerable narcissists tend to take a more subtle or emotionally manipulative approach. They may write passive-aggressive messages aimed at making other people feel guilty.

   For instance, a vulnerable narcissist may make a post about how lonely they are, or how they feel "no one cares." This is a kind of power play because it leaves their family and friends feeling as though they should make more of an effort to keep the narcissist happy.

4. *Attempts at ingratiating themselves with influencers or brands*
This is the online equivalent of name dropping. If someone repeatedly tries to get responses from famous people or companies, they may well be a narcissist looking to boost their social status. Be

especially cautious if they target high-end retailers or influencers who promote a lavish lifestyle.

5. *Posts that criticize or attack other people*
Narcissists are happy to criticize people in real life, so it should come as no surprise that they do it online. It's normal to express an opinion, but repeatedly putting people down, especially for relatively innocuous reasons, is a big red flag.

6. *Requests for shares or likes, with little or no reciprocation*
Unless they want to impress you—usually because they think you have some kind of power they'd like for themselves—they'd rather ask for shares instead of respond to what you've posted.

What About Online Dating?

Dealing with a narcissist on social media can be tiresome, but the stakes are higher if you meet them on a dating site.

Here are some big warning signs:

1. *They have an extremely long profile.*
Narcissists can, and do, talk about themselves for hours. If you stumble upon a profile that's really just a wall of text listing all their achievements, best qualities, and plans for the future, you might have found a narcissist.

Some people aren't great at writing about themselves and don't realize that people don't want to read long profiles, so don't be too quick to jump to conclusions. However, anyone who seems self-obsessed on their profile is probably the same in real life.

2. *They have a long list of things they expect in a partner.*
    Even if they aren't a good relationship candidate, a grandiose narcissist will believe they are entitled to a partner who meets their (very high) standards.

    A vulnerable narcissist might take a different approach. Instead of demanding that you live up to an unrealistic set of criteria, they might cast themselves in the role of an unloved, broken-hearted individual who just wants to find their soulmate.

    Any profile that contains some kind of "sob story" is suspect. At best, it suggests that the person who wrote it has some serious self-esteem issues. At worst, they may be trying to lure in sympathetic, naïve people who will lavish them with compliments and encouragement.

    Be on red alert if their profile challenges you to "prove them wrong" about women, men, or people in general. You'll never be good enough, and when you dare fall short of their high standards, you'll be on the receiving end of their anger and abuse.

3. *They send inappropriate messages.*
    Writing messages on dating sites is an art form. Striking the right tone and picking a good conversation starter is hard. However, most people know that sending excessively complimentary, sexual,

or lengthy messages isn't appropriate. If someone sends you strange messages that suggest they don't understand basic online etiquette or social norms, be on your guard.

At first, a narcissist's messages might make you feel good. Online dating can be time-consuming and frustrating. Stumbling across someone who appears sensitive, charming, and entertaining feels like a great stroke of luck. Unfortunately, they are probably sending similar messages to lots of people and waiting to see who takes the bait.

4. *Their profile contains a lot of selfies, most of which are half-naked.*

   We all want to know what our date actually looks like before meeting up with them, but narcissists often show just a little too much. A gym selfie or two is fine, but a gallery of filtered, posed shots styled like a fashion shoot is a big red flag.

   If you decide to go ahead and meet them anyway, don't be surprised if they look nothing like their profile photo. Narcissists aren't worried about representing themselves in a realistic light. They only want to lure you in to get the attention and approval they so desperately crave.

5. *They claim that they're in an open relationship, or that they are "non-monogamous."*

   Dating sites are the perfect hunting ground for a narcissist looking for attention outside their relationship. Even if their partner dotes on them, it might not be enough for their huge ego. Lots of narcissists don't see anything wrong with infidelity—at least, not when they're the ones cheating.

Open relationships are now more acceptable than ever before, with some dating sites even giving you the option to indicate that you're non-monogamous. This is useful for people in unconventional partnerships.

Unfortunately, it's also a great cover for narcissists. After all, if they tell you upfront that they aren't looking for an exclusive relationship, you can't expect them to be faithful. To the narcissist, this means they don't have to make the effort to get to know you. They like to have several romantic interests on the back burner, gathering attention from as many people as possible.

6. *Their quiz results suggest narcissistic tendencies.*
Some websites offer their members the chance to do personality tests or quizzes. Other members can then view the results. Of course, these are hardly in-depth psychological assessments, but they can provide you with clues as to someone's true self.

Watch out for anyone who has written lengthy, self-aggrandizing responses to quiz questions, or proudly displays personality test results that portray them in a negative light.

7. *You get the impression that they are holding something back.*

Smart people know that it's a bad idea to share too much personal information on a public profile. However, genuine, well-intentioned members will give a general overview of what they do for a living and how they fill their free time.

Some narcissists lead chaotic lives. They hide this on their profile by providing no information whatsoever about their studies or career. They might go into great detail about their plans or aspirations for the future but have no track record of actually succeeding at anything.

Some fill their profiles with complete lies. For instance, they might tell you they have their own home and a great career, whereas in fact they live in their mother's basement and occasionally do some casual work.

TRUST YOUR GUT

Perhaps you've met someone who isn't obviously a narcissist but still makes you feel ill at ease. That's your intuition speaking. Trust it! Sometimes, we can't put a finger on what's wrong with someone until much later. Don't hang around until you figure out why someone makes your alarm bells go off.

SUMMARY

- Learning how to identify narcissists is your best defense against them.
- You can spot a narcissist by observing how they speak to, and treat, those around them.
- Narcissists talk over others, demand special treatment, and generally behave in an obnoxious manner.
- Narcissists love using social media and dating sites to get attention. Stay vigilant when you're online.
- Better safe than sorry. If something doesn't seem right, trust your own judgment and move on.

CHAPTER 3:

SHIELDING YOURSELF FROM NARCISSISTS

To understand what makes someone irresistible to the average narcissist, we need to look at the issue from the narcissist's perspective. In this chapter, you'll discover the traits that leave you vulnerable to their abuse, and what you can do about it.

WHAT DOES THE TYPICAL NARCISSIST LOOK FOR?

Narcissists don't only go after shy, meek, self-effacing individuals. In fact, they may deliberately seek out people who are extremely successful professionally or socially because narcissists get a sick sense of satisfaction from controlling someone who appears "strong."

You may think that assertive, self-assured individuals would quickly cut a narcissist out of their lives. Unfortunately, some outwardly successful people are concealing unresolved hurts and trauma, and this makes them vulnerable to manipulation.

Sound familiar?

If you have any of the following characteristics, you need to remain especially vigilant:

1. *Low self-esteem*

   If you lack confidence, you are more likely to fall for a narcissist's empty praise. You'll be so relieved and excited that someone is paying you attention, that you won't slow down and check in with your gut.

2. *Empathy*

   Empaths, highly sensitive people (HSP), and all-around "good guys" (or gals) make a narcissist think, "Jackpot!" Empathetic people are keen to help others, and they often end up pouring a lot of time and effort into maintaining relationships with abusive people. In extreme cases, an empath can end up financially supporting a narcissist's lifestyle because they think the narcissist "just needs a bit of love and help."

3. *A willingness to give others second (and third) chances*

   Narcissists target kind, forgiving souls who want to give everyone the benefit of the doubt. They know they can get away with bad behavior because they will be given endless opportunities to redeem themselves.

4. *Loneliness*

   If you don't have many friends, or you've been single for a long time, hanging out with a narcissist can seem better than nothing. Narcissists have an uncanny knack for honing in on people who are desperate for companionship, knowing that they can exploit this natural human need.

5. *Little or no experience with positive, healthy relationships*
Most of us need to date, and spend time with, different types of people before we learn what separates good and bad relationships. That's natural. It's part of growing up. Unfortunately, if you lack experience with relationships, it's harder to spot narcissists.

Worse, if you're accustomed to bad relationships, you'll assume that narcissistic behavior is normal. Your family background also comes into play here. If your upbringing left you feeling that abuse and narcissism is just the price you pay for loving someone, you'll be vulnerable to narcissistic abuse as an adult.

6. *Good listening skills*
Nothing annoys a narcissist more than the feeling that nobody is listening to them. Bad listeners might be rude, but they do have one thing going for them—narcissists usually leave them alone. On the other hand, if you've been raised to let others talk, even if it means letting your own views go unheard, you'll be highly attractive to a narcissist.

7. *An inability to say "No"*
You need strong boundaries if you want to keep toxic people out of your life. Narcissists assume that

their preferences and demands should always come first. They think it's perfectly acceptable to ask others for favors. It comes naturally to them.

If you want to make other people like you, your default response to any request might be "Yes," or "Of course I'll do it!" At first, you may even feel good about granting favors, especially if you're the sort of person who likes to feel useful. Unfortunately, you'll slowly begin to realize that the narcissist is taking advantage of you. By then, you may have formed an emotional attachment to them that makes it hard to leave.

8. *A victim attitude*

    People who have been hurt or let down by others sometimes cope by adopting the role of victim or martyr. Unfortunately, a victim attitude will attract even more toxic people into your life. Why? Because narcissists can tell when you're using brittle defenses designed to keep people out. They know it won't take much effort to worm their way into your life, as long as they can tap into your vulnerabilities and exploit your personal hopes and dreams.

ARE YOU AN EMPATH?

It's a cruel irony that people who are the most easily hurt are often attracted to toxic individuals. If you are an empath, you have a lot of love to give. You are quick to assume the best of people and are sympathetic when someone shares their deepest feelings with you. In a healthy relationship, that's great!

Unfortunately, narcissists exploit empaths. They know an empath will be eager to support and help them, and they thrive on this narcissistic supply. In return, the empath will believe that their narcissistic friend or partner will show up as an equal partner in the relationship.

By the time the empath realizes who the narcissist truly is, they are hooked. Empaths and HSPs try to work hard at their relationships. They fool themselves into thinking that if only they give the narcissist more time and love, things will work out. This never happens because a narcissist doesn't reciprocate. Instead, they drain their empathetic or HSP partner dry, and then move onto their next victim.

HOW TO PROTECT YOURSELF FROM NARCISSISTS

1. *Grow your self-esteem.*

    When you value yourself, you stop looking to other people to give your life a sense of purpose. Good self-esteem isn't arrogance. It's about having a healthy appreciation for your traits and talents, celebrating your achievements, and forgiving yourself when you make a mistake.

    When you know that you are good enough just as you are, you'll be immune to a narcissist's empty praise. You'll also stop giving manipulative people second chances because you know that your time is too precious to waste on them.

Self-esteem can't be developed overnight. It's a long-term project. Start by taking an inventory of your skills and achievements and be sure to add to it over time. Ask a trusted friend or relative to remind you of all the good stuff you've done, and take pride in your accomplishments.

Learning something new can bolster your self-esteem. Try picking up a new hobby or going back to an old pastime you've been neglecting. Building new skills is self-affirming and empowering.

Change the way you talk to yourself. People with low self-esteem frequently pick on themselves and speak to themselves in a judgmental tone. The first step to kicking your inner critic is just to notice it. Let your inner voice "speak," but remind yourself that you don't need to accept whatever it says as true. As the saying goes, you don't have to believe everything you think.

If you can't seem to make any progress, it's time to talk to a therapist. Some of us have been through traumatic experiences or difficulties that have eroded our self-esteem. Talking to a professional can help you reprogram your mind to see yourself and your life in a new, more realistic light.

2. *Make friends with healthy role models.*
   When you hang out with unhealthy people, you start seeing bad behavior as normal. If you make friends with secure, well-rounded people with a firm grip on reality, your standards will rise.

Make a new rule for yourself: From now on, you will only make friends with people who have qualities you admire. Look for those who are honest, consistent, reliable, optimistic, and generally good-hearted. Watch out for anyone who is always negative, puts other people down, or doesn't seem to have any constructive hobbies or interests.

The best places to meet healthy people are public spaces where like-minded folks gather. Try meetup groups that match your interests, local adult education classes, the gym, places of worship, and workshops or events at your local community center.

You could also take a fresh look around your workplace. Have you been overlooking any potential friends? Is there someone you've always admired but haven't ever spoken to? It might be a good time to shore up your self-confidence and strike up a conversation.

3. *Take your relationships at the right speed.*
   Narcissists keep their victims distracted from their undesirable behaviors with a flurry of compliments. They also confide too much personal information far earlier than most other people would and expect the same of you in return. This leaves you vulnerable to manipulation because narcissists use your secrets and insecurities against you at a later stage.

   Don't dive straight into a new friendship or romantic relationship. If someone is right for you, they won't mind taking things at a sensible pace. Remember, you are under no obligation to be someone's friend or partner just because they show an interest in you. Be wary of anyone who tries to latch onto you too quickly or claims that they feel they've known you "forever."

4. *Build a good support network.*

When you have steady relationships with people who are willing to support you through bad times, you'll be less susceptible to narcissists. You won't be tempted to depend on toxic people for flattery or encouragement because you'll already have supportive friends that look out for you.

Take your relationships seriously. Nurture the people you care about, be there when they need your help, and spend quality time with them. If you have an argument with a loved one, reach out and make amends. There's no guarantee that treating people well will pay off, but you can't hope to grow a strong social network unless you put in the effort. If your social circle is small, make a plan to get out there and meet new people.

5. *Recognize and respect your own needs.*

If you don't decide what you will and won't tolerate in a relationship, other people will choose for you. You'll feel out of control and will attract toxic people who realize they can manipulate you.

We all have the same rights and needs. We all deserve respect, to feel safe, and to be heard. Unfortunately, lots of us believe that these rights are for everyone else, not us. It's time to start valuing yourself!

Draw up a charter of what you want and expect from a healthy relationship. You now have a list of standards that will help you identify whether someone else's behavior is acceptable. If you aren't sure where to start, have a look at this list of basic rights:

- The right to be listened to
- The right to change your mind
- The right to live free from fear and abuse
- The right to basic respect
- The right to spend time alone
- The right to pursue your own hobbies and interests
- The right to turn down unreasonable requests for favors
- The right to say "No" to anything that would harm you
- The right to hold your own religious and political beliefs without ridicule
- The right to privacy; for example, you don't have to answer overly personal questions
- The right to end a relationship whenever you want; you don't have to give a "good reason"

6. *Set and defend strong boundaries.*

    Although everyone has the same rights as a human being, your personal boundaries are unique. This is because we all have different desires and comfort levels when it comes to interacting with other people.

    For example, if you are an affectionate person, you might enjoy hugging your friends. However, it's perfectly OK if you are more reserved and only want to touch close relatives or your partner.

    Whatever your boundaries happen to be, you must learn how to communicate and defend them. Otherwise, you'll become frustrated and resentful when others deliberately or inadvertently trample over them.

    Narcissists will vigorously defend their own boundaries whilst ignoring everyone else's. You can't rely on them to behave with decency, so you need to practice standing up for yourself.

    It's time to make another list. This time write out your boundaries. To get started, think about the kind of behaviors you like and dislike in other people. Think about the best relationships and friendships you've ever had—then reflect on those that caused you the most pain. This will give you an insight into how you need others to behave.

    For example, if you have been in a relationship where someone smothered you, you might place special emphasis on drawing boundaries around how often someone gets to communicate with you.

Here are some examples of boundaries:

- "I only hug good friends, not acquaintances or people I don't know well."
- "I don't take phone calls after 8 p.m., unless it's an emergency."
- "I need at least an hour's notice if someone wants to visit."
- "I don't lend money to anyone."
- "I don't sleep with someone until they have agreed we are in an exclusive relationship."
- "If someone makes sexist or racist jokes in my presence, I call them out on it or leave the room."
- "If someone threatens me or makes me feel unsafe, I won't spend any more time with them."
- "If someone insults me, I remove myself from the situation and don't see that person again until they offer me an apology."

Your next task is to come up with some stock words and phrases you can use when someone tries to violate your boundaries.

If you're dealing with a narcissist, you'll need to be persistent and assertive to get your message across. Most people back off after being told "No" because they don't want to violate others' boundaries. Unfortunately, narcissists don't value your needs. You'll need to use a firmer approach.

Here are some useful phrases:

- "No, and that's my final answer."
- "Thanks for asking, but that doesn't work for me, so my answer is 'no.'"
- "That's an inappropriate question, and I'm not going to answer it."
- "My answer is 'No,' and it's not up for debate."

Do not offer explanations or justifications because this provides the narcissist with an opportunity to debate your response. As the saying goes, "No" is a complete sentence.

Use the Broken Record Technique to throw off a particularly insistent narcissist. Simply repeat your response, word for word, using precisely the same tone of voice, until they give up. This requires willpower because the narcissist may get annoyed or angry, making provocative statements that upset you.

You can also tell the narcissist what will happen if they don't respect your boundaries. Impose consequences for unacceptable behavior. For example, you could say, "If you don't stop insulting me, I'm going to go home." Note that you must follow through, or you will undermine your own credibility. Narcissists see empty threats as a sign of weakness.

7. *Educate yourself.*

Schools don't teach children how to spot narcissists. If you're lucky, someone might have sat you down and talked to you about toxic people, but most of us have to figure this stuff out for ourselves.

By reading this book, you're already educating yourself about narcissists and how they operate.

If you're interested in human behavior, take it further and invest in some psychology textbooks. Social psychologists have spent years researching how manipulative people work to get their own way, and reading up on their findings can be very illuminating.

TAKE IT SLOW

You don't have to master all these skills at once. Like everyone else, you are a work in progress. Every time you stand up for yourself or treat yourself well, pat yourself on the back. If making changes feels impossible, consider reaching out to a therapist who can help you get on the right track.

SUMMARY

- Some of us seem to attract more than our fair share of narcissistic individuals.
- Fortunately, you can identify what makes you attractive to narcissists and learn new skills to keep them at bay.

- Good self-esteem, strong relationships, and firm boundaries deter narcissists.
- Changing your self-image will take time, but it's worth the effort. You'll start attracting healthier people into your life, and you will feel much happier as a result.

CHAPTER 4:

WHAT TO DO WHEN YOUR PARENT IS A NARCISSIST

So far, we've covered general principles for dealing with narcissists. In the following chapters, we're going to look at how you can handle the narcissists you might have to deal with on an everyday basis. We'll begin with narcissistic parents.

HOW DO I KNOW WHETHER MY PARENT IS A NARCISSIST?

Do any of the following sound familiar?[13]

1. *As a child, you often had the feeling that your existence was an inconvenience.*

   Narcissists are so self-centered, their own children can be an annoyance. Your parent might have told you that having children made their life so much harder or warned you against having children of your own because they take up so much time, effort, and money.

This attitude might also have come through in their behavior. For example, they might have chosen to go out all the time, leaving you in the care of babysitters. They may have given you the impression that they'd rather be doing almost anything else than spend time with you.

According to psychologist Seth Mayers, narcissists don't have children because they want to nurture and support another human being. Instead, having a child serves as a form of narcissistic supply because the parent-child relationship has a built-in power imbalance.[14]

Because a child is dependent on their parents, the narcissist who has a child is guaranteed the chance to manipulate someone else for many years. Children also offer them a chance to gain status in the community, especially if they can raise "successful" children or convince everyone around them that they are a model parent with a happy family.

2. *Your parent often bragged about your achievements (real or exaggerated) to other people.*

    Narcissists regard their children as an extension of themselves. From their perspective, a child who does well is a source of pride and an "average" child is a source of embarrassment. Narcissists use their children as a means of living out their own dreams and fantasies. Your parent may have boasted to anyone who would listen about how smart or talented you are and pushed you to excel in fields and activities you didn't even enjoy.

For example, perhaps you didn't like dancing, but your parent always wanted to be a dancer and so pushed you to attend lessons and compete in shows.

3. *Your parent cast you in the role of their confidante and asked for a lot of reassurance or made it clear that you should be taking care of them.*

   If your parent was a vulnerable narcissist, they may have parentified you. "Parentification" is a term used to describe a kind of role reversal in which a parent looks for emotional support from a child who isn't old enough to understand adult problems.

   For example, if your parent's relationship was in trouble, they may have burdened you with all the details instead of turning to a friend or therapist. In some cases, narcissistic parents parentify their children because they don't have a support network willing to listen. More often, they regard their child as their personal counselor and emotional sponge.

4. *Your parent found it difficult to control their temper, and their mood swings were so extreme that they left you feeling worried or unsafe.*

   Parenting is tough. Children, through no fault of their own, can be frustrating at times. Narcissists, who have thin skins and tend to take everything personally, find it hard to keep their tempers in check.

Your parent may have acted or responded in inappropriate ways. For example, they might have shouted and screamed when you made a tiny mistake or had an accident.

Narcissists can experience moments of elation or excessive self-confidence. These mood swings don't always have an obvious trigger, and this can be alarming for a young child.

5. *Communication in your family was never clear.*
Narcissistic parents don't sit down with their children or spouse to address problems in a calm, constructive manner. Instead, they resort to passive-aggressive tactics, pointed comments, or fits of rage.

It's common for them to complain about someone to a third party, sit back, and wait for gossip to spread. This gives a narcissist a sense of control over a situation and lets them fulfill their need to manipulate others.

As a result, everyone starts feeling suspicious of one another.[15] If you never felt as though you could have a straightforward conversation with your parent without causing drama, they may be a narcissist.

6. *Your parent had unrealistic standards.*
Because your successes or failures reflected directly on them, your parent may have told you from an early age that anything less than perfection wasn't an option. You might have been punished for getting a B instead of an A on your report card or

chastised because you weren't the prettiest or thinnest one in your friendship group.

7. *Your parent was very controlling when you were a child. They may have tried to dictate your hobbies, what clothes you wore, who you saw, what major you picked in college, and so on.*

Narcissists don't like to think of their children as humans with their own preferences. As a result, they try to influence every aspect of their children's lives.

8. *As a child, you felt that your parent only loved you conditionally.*

Perhaps you never felt loved and respected for being yourself. Your parent may have shown you warmth and affection, but only when you did exactly as they wished. You may have resorted to rebellious or even self-destructive behavior in a bid to see whether they'd accept you when you weren't playing the role of the perfect child.

9. *You were reluctant to invite friends to your house because you didn't want them to meet your parent.*

Young children don't know what "narcissist" means, but that doesn't mean they can't tell something isn't quite right. From an early age, you might have realized that your parent wasn't "normal" and may have felt awkward or embarrassed when they met your friends.

10. *Your parent was charming to everyone outside your home but turned into someone else behind closed doors.*

    Narcissists lead double lives. Many are absolutely charming to people they don't know very well, and some can even sustain friendships. However, their families know them to be quite different. Their children see the worst of their behavior. You might have grown up feeling confused as to why your parent could be so nice and considerate towards everyone but you.

11. *Your parent's memories and perceptions didn't line up with your own.*

    Living with a narcissist is crazy-making. Because they lack empathy, they don't understand how their actions hurt others. From their perspective, they should never be held accountable.

    When you try to tell a narcissist how their behaviors make you feel, they will deny the reality of your feelings, tell you that you're just overreacting, or blame you for the incident. They are masters at throwing things back in your face. If you confront them with evidence, they will ignore you, claim not to remember what happened, or tell you that you've misunderstood the whole situation. This is known in therapy circles as "gaslighting."

    Children raised by narcissists report that they were made to feel as though their perceptions were wrong. If you often felt that your parent didn't want to listen to your side of the story, or got mad at you for telling the truth, they might be a narcissist.

12. *Your parent encouraged you to compete against your siblings and other relatives.*

Under normal circumstances, a parent encourages all their children to get along. Not so in families headed by narcissistic parents, who actively promote competition and rivalry. The parent will do this for two reasons.

First, damaging the relationship between siblings makes it less likely that they will join together to challenge their parent's inappropriate behavior. Second, pitting children against one another can drive each to push harder, thereby racking up more achievements and trophies for the narcissist to brag about.

NOT ALL NARCISSISTIC PARENTS ARE THE SAME

No two narcissistic parents are identical. It's unlikely you will recognize all the signs listed here, and it's also unlikely that you'll ever convince your parent to undergo psychiatric evaluation to get a diagnosis.

What matters is how you feel about your own experience. If you sincerely believe that your parent is a narcissist, they probably are.

THE LEGACY OF BEING RAISED BY A NARCISSISTIC PARENT

Being subjected to narcissistic abuse for many years warps your sense of self. Children of narcissists need to understand how their experiences may affect them later in life.

Facing up to these consequences is painful. The good news is that, if you were raised by a narcissist, you can heal. You can learn to enjoy positive relationships, nurture yourself, and grow your self-esteem.

Adult children of narcissists often have the following problems:

1. *Trouble with setting and defending boundaries*
    Narcissistic parents don't respect their children's privacy. They feel entitled to know precisely what their children are thinking, feeling, and doing at all times. Your narcissistic parent might have read your diary, listened in on your phone calls, or barged into your room without knocking.

    As an adult, the idea that you can—and should—decide how involved other people can be in your life might feel alien. You may feel you have no right to walk away from toxic people and situations.

2. *Problems with developing healthy relationships and picking healthy partners*
    If your family relationships were based on mutual respect, you will grow up with a healthy set of expectations for friendships and romantic relationships.

Children raised by narcissists don't have positive role models. They grow up thinking that it's normal for people to claim they love you yet criticize you at every turn. They are more likely to choose toxic partners and accept inappropriate behavior as normal and OK.

3. *Low self-esteem*

Children who don't receive consistent affection and validation from their parents often grow up with low self-esteem. You may be unsure whether you are really worthy of love or find it hard to believe that anyone could want to befriend or date you.

You might carry the sense of never being "quite good enough," which can get you into trouble if you are always trying to earn validation from others.

4. *Problems trusting their own feelings*

If your narcissistic parent dismissed your feelings or belittled your wants and desires, you might have grown into an adult who mistrusts your own emotions.

5. *A tendency to put other peoples' needs ahead of their own*

To survive, some children raised by narcissists learn how to accommodate their parent's feelings. Children are vulnerable and dependent on their parents, so it's safest to obey them. In the short term, this is a good tactic because it can placate a narcissist.

Unfortunately, these children often carry this tendency into adulthood. If you are used to tiptoeing around your mother or father, you might automatically assume that you need to behave similarly in every relationship. Over time, you might notice that your needs always seem to come second to everyone else's.

6. *Difficult relationships with siblings and other family members*
Chaotic, toxic households don't foster healthy relationships. This manifests itself in various ways. For example, children of narcissists who have been encouraged to compete against their siblings rarely have the chance to get to know their brothers or sisters as individuals.

7. *Problems with substance abuse and other self-destructive behaviors*
If your childhood experiences contributed to your depression or anxiety as an adult, you may turn to alcohol, drugs, or other forms of self-harm in a bid to escape your psychological pain.

How To Deal With Your Narcissistic Parent

Realizing that your parent is a narcissist can come as a great relief. Learning about NPD parents will help you understand why your childhood was so difficult and the effects it may still be having on you as an adult.

But how can you cope with the fallout, which can last a lifetime? How should you handle your parent now that you've grown up? We'll address these questions in the next chapter.

SUMMARY

- Narcissistic parents don't view their children as individuals but as extensions of themselves.
- If your parent was a narcissist, they probably undermined your confidence, made you feel insecure, and failed to provide you with the love and stability you needed.
- As an adult child of a narcissist, you may have mental health problems and trouble forming positive relationships.

CHAPTER 5:

HOW TO HEAL FROM NARCISSISTIC PARENTING

I n this chapter, you'll learn about the stages you can expect to go through when coming to terms with your past as the child of a narcissistic parent. You'll learn how to get the right kind of support and how to reparent yourself.

HEALING FROM A NARCISSISTIC PARENT

You must learn how to trust yourself. For someone raised by a narcissist, this a major undertaking. When you've spent years being told that your feelings and perceptions are wrong, it takes courage to do this kind of work.

You'll need to trust your own memory. You can't rely on your parent to tell you what your childhood was really like. A narcissist will distort reality to suit their narrative. If you point out that they abused you, they are more likely to respond with anger, or they may guilt you into changing the subject.

Some people can work through past issues and trauma alone or with the aid of self-help books. However, you might need to talk to a professional therapist if your past is having a big impact on your day-to-day life. There's absolutely no shame in getting an outside perspective. It's a sign of strength to reach out to someone else.

THE STAGES OF HEALING

According to therapist Christine Hammond, it's normal to go through several stages when you decide to confront your past as a child of a narcissist.[16]

1. *Recognizing that something is deeply wrong*
    Your journey towards acceptance and healing actually started many years ago. As a child, you might not have had the vocabulary to describe what was going on at home, but you knew something wasn't right. As children of narcissistic parents reach adolescence, then adulthood, they realize that their family dynamic is not normal or positive.

2. *Studying narcissism*
    If you picked up this book because you have a suspicion that your parent is a narcissist, you are probably at this stage. You will want to read and listen to as much material on narcissism as you can. Coming to terms with the fact that you were raised by someone with these traits isn't easy, but it can be an enormous relief to finally have a term that describes your parent.

3. *Recounting the past and identifying key themes*

The next step is to evaluate your childhood and adolescence. Think about the times when your parent's narcissistic behaviors showed up. It can be helpful to take each of the key NPD criteria and map them accordingly. For example, if your parent's favorite topic of conversation was their own achievements and unrealistic aspirations, this points to grandiose narcissism.

Step 3 is emotionally draining. It can trigger some memories that you usually keep locked away. You might realize that you have been left with trauma that still impacts your adult life.

Not all abuse is physical. It can be verbal, sexual, financial, emotional, or even spiritual, if your parent uses their religious beliefs as a cover for their inappropriate behavior. At this stage, you may want to look for a therapist who can help you come to terms with abusive events from your past.

4. *Grieving what you never had*

As you start to confront the reality of your situation, you'll move through the five phases of grief: denial, anger, bargaining, depression, and acceptance. At first, you may find it hard to believe that your parent is a narcissist or that their behavior has had a big effect on your life.

Once you acknowledge the damage they have done, it's natural to feel angry. You may wonder why someone who supposedly loved you would treat you so badly. Next comes the bargaining phase. You may spend hours worrying that you just weren't "good enough," and if you'd only been a better child, they would have been more loving.

As you will come to realize, this is an illusion. The problem is with the narcissist, not you. When you understand that you can't change your parent, you'll feel empowered. At the same time, you might also feel depressed. If you've been clinging to any hope that they might change, you will need to release it. Only then can you reach acceptance.

5. *Personal growth*

At this point, you are in a great position to analyze your thoughts and beliefs about the world, relationships, and yourself. Perhaps your narcissistic parent left you with some toxic beliefs, such as "Status is what really matters," or "People are either winners or losers, and there is no in-between."

With your newfound self-awareness, you can choose to challenge your worldview and change the way you speak to yourself. For example, if you recognize that you tend to speak to yourself harshly whenever you make a mistake, it's time to learn how to support and encourage yourself instead.

6. *Forgiveness*

You are under no obligation whatsoever to forgive an abusive or narcissistic parent. However, true forgiveness can be healing. Forgiveness doesn't mean that you approve of what your parent did. Neither does it mean that you need to maintain a relationship with them.

Healthy forgiveness is most beneficial for the forgiver, not the person who has done wrong. Forgiving someone means that you no longer dwell on the past. You accept what has happened, and you release any feelings of righteous indignation. It can take a long time, so don't rush this part of the process.

Some people find that understanding their narcissistic parent's past can help. For instance, if someone discovers that their abusive mother or father was abused at a young age, they may start to feel some empathy towards them.

On the other hand, it's important to note that personal experience of abuse is never a justification for abusing anyone else. No matter how sad your parent's past, they had no good reason whatsoever to mistreat you. Don't let anyone guilt you into forgiving them just because they had a rough start in life.

ARE YOUR CURRENT RELATIONSHIPS HEALTHY?

Take an honest look at your friendships and romantic relationships. Have you been seeking out people who resemble your narcissistic parent? Human beings tend to seek out what they already know. You might feel comfortable with people who walk all over your feelings and dominate you at every opportunity.

You don't necessarily have to end a relationship with someone just because they have a few narcissistic tendencies. After all, narcissism occurs on a spectrum, and it's almost impossible to find someone completely free of narcissistic traits.

Focus on how a relationship makes you feel, rather than how many narcissistic traits the other person has. Do they make you feel safe, respected, and happy to be alive? If not, it's time to review the bill of rights in Chapter 3 and decide whether it's really worth continuing with the relationship.

REPARENTING YOURSELF

Accepting that you did not receive the love and nurturing that you deserved is part of the healing process.

All children deserve to feel loved and supported. They are all entitled to parents who try their best to meet their emotional needs. You may feel short-changed because you were deprived of a normal childhood and healthy role models. You have every right to feel this way. Negative childhood experiences can be devastating.

As an adult, you can't turn back the clock, but you can learn to reparent yourself. You can choose to learn new coping mechanisms to deal with sadness, anger, and other overpowering emotions. You can learn to practice self-love and unconditional self-acceptance.

Note that this doesn't mean you have to become a narcissist yourself. There is a huge difference between narcissism and healthy self-respect. If you have trouble separating the two, working with a therapist with experience in this area can help.

So, what exactly does reparenting look like?

Therapist Linda Esposito recommends these steps:[17]

1. *Take care of yourself on a basic level.*

   Eat well, exercise regularly, and take care of your home. Your mother or father might not have insisted you brush your teeth or eat your vegetables, but that doesn't mean you can't care for yourself as an adult. Nurture yourself on a psychological and intellectual level by developing your own interests.

2. *Practice mindfulness.*

   It's easy to get caught up in your memories or find yourself ruminating on the ways your parents failed you. You are completely justified in feeling angry, but getting bogged down in your negative thoughts and feelings will stop you living in the present. Mindfulness exercises and yoga will keep you calm and grounded.

3. *Decide on your boundaries and implement them in your day-to-day life.*

   Parents should teach their child the difference between acceptable and unacceptable behaviors, and how to defend themselves against people who wish them harm. If your parents fell short in this area, you need to learn more about your rights in relationships, and then be willing to stand up for the treatment you deserve.

4. *Stay mindful of how you treat other people and learn how to calm yourself down.*

   Your suffering doesn't give you a license to treat other people badly. To form healthy relationships with others, pay attention to how your actions and words affect your relationships. In Esposito's words, don't let yourself throw "adult temper tantrums."

5. *Take a cautiously optimistic view of the world.*

   In healthy parent-child relationships, the child learns that the world can be scary, but it is still a generally safe place. Growing up in a negative environment can leave you with an unnecessarily pessimistic worldview. Yes, there is much suffering in the world, but there is also a lot of joy. Let yourself notice and appreciate the good in people you meet.

FIND A SUPPORT GROUP

People who weren't raised by narcissists can't fully appreciate what you went through as a child. They may say well-meaning things like, "Oh yeah, my mother's difficult too, I know what that's like!" They are trying to be helpful, but their words can feel invalidating.

If you are seeing a therapist, ask them to recommend a support group. There are also charities and organizations that specialize in helping adult children of abusive parents, so Google local meetups in your area.

You can also join online forums for people who are working on coming to terms with their pasts. Just be careful when taking advice from other community members. They have valuable lived experience, but they are not usually mental health professionals. Likewise, don't be too quick to jump in with advice or suggestions when others share their problems.

THE NEXT STEP

Understanding the past is a big leap forward on your journey to healing from narcissistic abuse, but it isn't the only piece of the puzzle. Unless you have already cut contact with your family, you'll need to learn how to deal with their toxic behaviors on an ongoing basis. In the next chapter, we'll look at how you can handle narcissistic parents in your day-to-day life.

SUMMARY

- Coming to terms with your experiences as the child of a narcissist is a complex journey in which you move from recognition to acceptance.
- Stay vigilant in your relationships because children of narcissists tend to re-enact their parent-child dynamics.
- Learn to reparent yourself and make your own wellbeing a key priority in your life.
- Getting the right support will help you move forward.

CHAPTER 6:

SETTING NEW BOUNDARIES WITH PARENTS & OTHER NARCISSISTIC FAMILY MEMBERS

Narcissists don't spontaneously become good parents when you grow up and leave home. Unless you cut contact completely, you'll be dealing with their manipulative behaviors for the rest of your life. The sooner you learn how to handle them, the better.

This chapter focuses on parents, but most of these principles also apply to siblings, cousins, grandparents, and other family members.

STANDING UP TO YOUR NARCISSISTIC PARENT

We've already addressed the topic of boundaries in this book, but how should you use them when dealing with a narcissistic parent? Even if you know on an intellectual level that your mother or father has a personality disorder, changing the way you relate to them is tough.

Here are a few tips:[18]

1. *When you need to lay down a boundary, rehearse what you are going to say in advance.*

   For example, let's say your mother calls you every Sunday evening. These chats normally start off fine but quickly descend into petty arguments and name calling if you dare say something she doesn't like. You may decide that you will no longer tolerate being spoken to in such a disrespectful manner.

   Practice calling out the behavior, explaining how it makes you feel, and telling your parent what will happen if they violate your boundary in the future. Follow through if necessary.

   For example:

   > "Mom, I don't like it when you insult me. It makes me feel upset and belittled. If you insult me in the future when we're on the phone, I'm going to hang up."

   Aim for an assertive tone of voice. There is no need to be aggressive and aggravate the situation. Your aim is to set out your boundaries not provoke a fight.

2. *Do not allow yourself to be drawn into negotiations.*

   You do not have to explain your decisions to your parent, no matter how much they shout, whine, or accuse you of being selfish.

   This is a big task when you've been raised by a narcissist. As a child, your parent was in a position of absolute power. You were trapped at home, and they had all the time in the world to wear you down. However, as an adult, you have the ability to stop engaging and leave the room or put down the phone if necessary. Unless you are living in your parent's home or financially dependent on them, you can afford to walk away.

Your parent won't take kindly to your new boundaries. They have always assumed that they had the right to control you. Up until now, their efforts have been working. They are in for a rude awakening, and they won't be happy about it.

3. *Keep your expectations realistic.*

It's easy to fantasize that, when you start standing up for yourself, your parent will realize the error of their ways. This isn't going to happen. Boundaries protect your mental health and shield you from the worst of your parent's behaviors and attitudes. They are powerful tools. However, there is nothing magic about them, and they won't change your parent's personality.

When you change the status quo, their behavior may get worse as they attempt to regain control. As hard as it is to remember, their feelings are not your problem. Your parent is an adult, and their emotions are their responsibility.

SETTING BOUNDARIES WITH NARCISSISTIC IN-LAWS

Dealing with your own parents is one thing, but what if your partner has a narcissistic parent or sibling?

Narcissistic in-laws can make your life a misery. They might:

1. *Make frequent surprise visits to your home.*

   Most people realize that it's rude to drop by unannounced and expect a warm welcome. However, your narcissistic in-law may believe that this social rule doesn't apply to them.

2. *Make unreasonable demands on your partner's time.*

   Healthy people realize that adult children have their own lives. Narcissistic in-laws, on the other hand, assume that their children should prioritize them over everyone else, even a spouse. They may demand that your partner visit them every weekend, for example.

3. *Criticize you, your partner, or both of you for no good reason.*

   They may use criticism to make you feel insecure and to make themselves feel powerful.

4. *Try to tell you how to live your life, for example by telling you when to have children or how to decorate your house.*

   Narcissists believe they know best, so they won't hesitate to order you around. If you challenge them, they'll tell you that they are only trying to help. They may get mad and tell you how ungrateful you are.

5. *Tell you that you aren't good enough for their son or daughter.*

   In extreme cases, a narcissistic in-law may try to drive the two of you apart. One common tactic is to sow insecurity in your relationship by repeatedly telling you that their son or daughter could "do better." They may talk about your partner's exes in glowing terms, implying that you are a disappointment by comparison.

6. *Make family occasions awkward with their petty demands and love of drama.*

   Birthdays, anniversaries, even cookouts—a narcissist will somehow manage to make it all about them. Whether they're throwing a tantrum or making snide remarks to other guests, you can be sure that they'll draw attention to themselves.

7. *Pry into your personal affairs.*

   You and your partner need to be careful when it comes to sharing intimate details about your relationship. A narcissistic in-law may be adept at playing the role of a supportive relative, but they will be quick to use sensitive information against you when they want to manipulate you.

GETTING YOUR PARTNER ON BOARD

You'll need to choose and defend your personal boundaries, but you'll also need to make sure your partner supports you. The two of you need to work as a team. If you don't present a united front, your in-law won't take you seriously.

If your partner seems unhappy or reluctant to stand up to their relatives, try not to assume that they don't care about your feelings. They may have decided that the best—or only—way they can cope with their family member is to go along with their wishes.

If the two of you only have to see your in-laws occasionally, this strategy might be good enough. Unfortunately, if you have to deal with them on a frequent basis, you need to sit down and have a frank discussion about what you will and will not tolerate.

You might need to make a few compromises. For example, you may feel that seeing your in-laws every other weekend for a few hours is enough, but your partner might want to go every Sunday. You could agree to accompany them on alternate weekends and accept that they will always visit their family every week.

Trouble with in-laws can be a big problem. Some couples end up divorcing because they can't agree on how to handle these issues. Don't be ashamed to seek couple's therapy if it's causing a rift in your relationship. A good therapist can help you work out what you can expect from your narcissistic in-law, and how to implement boundaries as a couple.

Do You Have An Enabling Parent?

Unless you are unlucky enough to have two narcissistic parents, you were probably raised by a narcissist who was partnered with an enabler. If your parent found it hard to sustain any kind of romantic relationship, they may have gone through several partners during your childhood.

An enabler is someone who tolerates, or even encourages, someone else's bad behavior.

Your enabling parent, or partner, might have done the following:

1. *Made excuses for your narcissistic parent*
    They might have dismissed your concerns or told you that your parent "can't help" the way they are.

2. *Acted in a way that suggested they were scared of your narcissistic parent*
    Living with a narcissist is scary. The enabler may have quietly obeyed their partner just to keep the peace.

3. *Supported your narcissistic parent's behaviors one day yet tried to stand up to them the next*
    An enabler is trapped in a difficult position. They usually know that their partner's behavior towards the children is unacceptable, and sometimes they find the courage to challenge them. On the other hand, they might also try to preserve their own safety by keeping quiet or even supporting the narcissist.

4. *Spent a lot of time away from the family home in a bid to avoid their narcissistic partner*

   Perhaps they took a job that allowed them to travel for work or took up an engrossing hobby that gave them a reason to get out of the house.

5. *Became annoyed or angry when you asked them to explain your narcissistic parent's behaviors*

   Enablers sometimes find it hard to talk about their partner's behavior because it forces them to confront the reality of their situation. In some cases, they prefer to stay in denial. They don't want to acknowledge that they made a poor choice of partner or face up to their children's pain and suffering.

6. *Had affairs*

   People have affairs for many different reasons. Sometimes, they get romantically involved with someone else because they aren't getting validation or affection from their partner. If your enabling parent had an affair, they might have been trying to distract themselves from the state of their primary relationship.

HOW TO HANDLE YOUR ENABLING PARENT

Dealing with an enabling parent is a complicated problem. On one hand, they might have shielded you from the worst of your narcissistic parent's abuse. At the same time, they may also have encouraged or tolerated their partner's behavior, which means they were a secondary abuser.

Enabling partners are victims, yet also have autonomy. They may have been mentally abused to the point they feel dependent on the narcissist, but they could, and should, have chosen differently when it came to their own behavior.

Should you confront an enabler, and tell them how their behavior has affected you? It's a deeply personal decision, and the right answer will depend on your individual circumstances and ability to tolerate conflict.

Bear in mind that the conversation is more likely to go well if your parent and the enabler have broken up because the enabler will have less to lose by being honest with you. If they still live together, the enabler might become defensive. They may worry that their life will become difficult if they speak out against their narcissistic partner.

Leaving a narcissist is hard. It's emotionally draining and potentially dangerous. If your enabling parent is psychologically or financially dependent on their partner, they are unlikely to end the relationship.

Later in this book, you'll learn why it's so hard to exit a romantic relationship or marriage to a narcissist, which may help you understand why the enabler chose, or has chosen, to stay with your narcissistic parent.

WHEN TO CUT OFF CONTACT WITH YOUR NARCISSISTIC PARENT

Do you suspect that your life would be a lot easier if you had no contact with your parent? You may be right. Some children of narcissists choose to avoid their parent entirely.[19]

The main advantage of this strategy is that it clears away a lot of emotional noise from your life. You won't have to navigate a difficult parent-child relationship, and you'll be free of someone who puts you down, belittles you, and insists on trying to violate your boundaries. After the initial adjustment phase, you'll feel as though a big weight has been lifted from your shoulders.

On the other hand, the no contact route isn't something to be considered lightly. If your parents are still together and only one is a narcissist, you need to ask yourself whether you are happy to sever contact with them both. You could keep lines of communication open with your non-narcissistic parent, but this could put a strain on their relationship with the narcissist.

You also need to think about how going no contact will affect your relationships with your siblings, cousins, and other relatives. If you are lucky, they will understand why you've taken this step —but you should still be prepared for pushback. You may feel lonely, misunderstood, or even attacked. Because narcissists are great at manipulating others, everyone else might be fooled into thinking that you are the bad guy. This is a painful situation, and you may not want to put yourself through it.[20]

Finally, you should be prepared for your parent's narcissistic behaviors to escalate once they realize that you aren't communicating with them anymore. They may send you aggressive or whiny messages or call your phone multiple times per day.

They might recruit other people—"flying monkeys"—to tell you how much your parent misses you, how you have betrayed your family, or other sentiments designed to manipulate you into reinstating contact. Often, flying monkeys are well-meaning. They are trying to restore a broken relationship, not realizing that the situation was abusive.

You'll need to remain strong and remind yourself why you've chosen this path. It's normal to find yourself going back to your parent a few times before you make the final break. However badly our parents treat us, it's still natural to seek their approval and attention.

When Your Narcissistic Parent Passes On

You might assume that when a narcissistic parent dies, their children breathe a sigh of relief and swiftly move on with their lives. In some cases, this is exactly what happens.

Unfortunately, for most children of narcissists, things are a bit more complicated than that.[21] When your parent dies, you might feel a range of emotions.

1. *Deep, unexpected grief that leaves you feeling confused*
   However unpleasant, abusive, or toxic your parent was, they were still your mother or father. It's natural to mourn their loss, even if they abused you for a long time.

2. *Anger*
   When your parent dies, you may feel angry that they have "gotten away with it." In death, they are no longer accountable for their actions.

As the person left behind, you still have to deal with the fallout of your relationship. You may feel resentful that you are still carrying an emotional burden.

3. *Loneliness*

    Because narcissists are often superficially charming to people outside their own families, you might get lots of cards, letters, and floral arrangements from people who assume you've lost a much-loved parent. This can make you feel conflicted, guilty, and misunderstood.

4. *Guilt*

    You may wonder whether you should have done more to repair the relationship. Don't be surprised if you find yourself thinking "coulda, woulda, shoulda" thoughts.

5. *Emptiness*

    When your parent dies, you may find that you have a lot more time and energy. Suddenly, you realize how much of your life was taken up by thinking about, and managing, your narcissistic mother or father. As strange as it sounds, you might feel disorientated.

HANDLING YOUR NARCISSISTIC PARENT WHEN YOU HAVE CHILDREN

If you have children, managing your relationship with a narcissistic parent becomes even more complicated. There're lots of issues to navigate.[22] For example, how can you make sure they respect your parenting style? Can they be trusted with babysitting duties? Are they likely to start bullying or mistreating your children and, if so, what on earth should you do?

A narcissistic grandparent will often want to be involved in their grandchildren's lives. That's all well and good, but it's likely they won't respect your boundaries. For example, they may offer your kids candy every time you visit, even if you tell them that your children only get candy on special occasions. You'll need to draw on your best boundary setting skills, otherwise they will learn that they do whatever they like with no repercussions.

Some narcissists are abusive towards their own children but excessively nice to their grandkids. If you are the child in question, this can be hard to swallow. Part of you might be wondering, "Why weren't they that nice to me when I was growing up?"

Remember that the role of parent and grandparent are very different. Grandparents usually have less responsibility for the child and feel that it's their right (or even duty) to spoil them. This is normal, even in healthy families.

If you decide that your parent is a toxic influence on your child, it might be best to reduce or eliminate contact altogether. This works best if your partner is completely on board with your decision, particularly if the narcissist in question is their mother or father. However, be aware that your child will probably be curious about their grandparents, especially as they get older. Be honest. Children can sense when adults are lying, and they will hold it against you later.

SUMMARY

- If you want to stay in contact with your narcissistic parent, you'll need to consistently implement boundaries.
- You may have to come to terms with the fact that your other parent enables their partner's narcissism.
- In some cases, cutting contact altogether may be the best solution.
- Sometimes the death of a narcissistic parent is a relief, but it can also trigger some complex feelings.
- Narcissistic in-laws can make your life very difficult unless you and your partner work together to deal with their behavior.
- Some narcissists can be a positive force in their grandchildren's lives, but the grandchild-grandparent relationship requires careful management.

CHAPTER 7:

ARE YOU DATING A NARCISSIST?

I f you are already involved with someone who has pathological narcissism or NPD, you need to make some important choices. You don't necessarily need to call the
relationship to a halt, but it's wise to educate yourself about
the common moves narcissists pull and how to respond. In
this chapter, we'll look at how narcissists approach dating,
love, and sex.

THE TELLTALE SIGNS

We've already seen how you can spot narcissists in your day-
to-day life, but there are specific signs you should watch for
if you're in, or are looking for, a romantic relationship.

1.   *The more you listen to them, the more loving they are.*
     The more narcissistic supply you provide, the more
     affection and approval they give you. Their idea of
     the perfect partner is someone who will pump up
     their ego whilst boosting their status in the eyes of
     others.

2. *They need a stream of compliments, and they want you to acknowledge their greatness when you're with other people.*[23]

   In a healthy relationship, both partners feel they can give one another constructive criticism. If you're dating a narcissist, anything other than un-conditional adoration will elicit contempt, silence, or rage.

3. *They allow themselves to be an imperfect partner but criticize you if you make a tiny mistake.*

   In the narcissist's eyes, they are above the law, and the normal rules of a relationship don't apply to them. For example, they might flirt with someone else at a party and expect you to overlook it but become angry if you were to do the same. In short, they are hypocritical.

4. *They can't share in your joy when something goes well in your life.*

   Your partner should be your biggest supporter. When you get a new job, buy a home, or win an award, they should be happy for you. Narcissists struggle with this because they need to feel like "the best" or the most successful one in the relationship.

   They may belittle your achievements or feign disinterest because acknowledging them would be too threatening to their ego. They might accuse you of being big-headed or arrogant, knowing that if they make you feel guilty, you will stay quiet.

5. *They are very generous with gifts and time, but only at the beginning of a relationship.*

    Narcissists are skilled in the art of sweeping people off their feet. Think back to the start of your relationship. Did everything seem a little too good to be true? Did you feel really lucky to have found someone who just so happened to share all your interests and hopes for the future?

    Narcissists attract potential partners by mirroring them. They quickly hone in on what you want to hear. They then parrot it back to you, along with grand romantic gestures. This is an intoxicating combination that will get you hooked.

    Later, you might discover that the narcissist has no interest in your hobbies and doesn't share your long-term goals. Unfortunately, by this point, you may have already developed strong feelings that make it hard to let go of the relationship. The narcissist can take full advantage of your love for them, using you as a source of narcissistic supply until they get bored and move on.

6. *They listen to your problems, but they don't seem to understand your feelings.*

    If it benefits them to do so, a narcissist can put on a good show of listening to you. For example, if they are still in the early stages of a relationship and want you to think that they are kind and caring, they may listen as you tell them about your terrible day at work. But a narcissist cannot really show any meaningful level of empathy.

You may get the impression that they are just going through the motions, nodding occasionally whilst staring into the distance. In time, when the narcissist has "won" you over, they'll probably stop pretending to listen and shut you down instead.

7. *You catch yourself making excuses for their bad behavior.*
    It's normal to see your loved one through rose-tinted glasses. It's not necessarily a bad thing. Positive bias makes it easier to live with another human being. However, when you start overlooking red flags and destructive behaviors because you're desperate to hold onto the relationship, it's time to take a step back.

8. *You start noticing inconsistencies in their stories, or you come across evidence that they've been lying to you.*
    With their unhealthy self-image and distorted view of the world, narcissists don't generally have a strong grasp of reality. They may also change their version of events to impress you or lull you into a false sense of security. They might give you a false version of events to trick you into thinking that they have been victimized in order to gain sympathy.

    For example, they might tell you that their ex was "crazy" or "abusive" so that you'll feel sorry for them. However, in time, you may learn from other sources that their ex was actually the one on the receiving end of the narcissist's abuse.

Narcissists may even get a kick out of deceiving you for the sake of it because it gives them a sense of power. For instance, your partner might tell you that they were at the gym after work, when they were actually out having drinks with a work colleague. A few days later, they may then let slip a comment about the bar they visited.

9. *They make promises but fail to follow through.*[24]

Does your partner promise to take you on a date, but then "forgets" to book a table? Do they promise to be a better listener, but still prefer to look at their phone every night at the dinner table instead of giving you their full attention?

Remember, narcissists are self-serving. They don't bother staying true to their word unless it helps them get what they want. So, your partner may go to the trouble of arranging a dinner date if they think they will get sex in return, but they are unlikely to make the effort if the only reward is your happiness.

10. *They make you jealous.*[25]

Narcissists keep their partners on edge by talking about their exes in glowing terms, by making it clear that they find other people attractive, or saying that it would be great to date other people. They might subtly (or not so subtly) compare you to their former partners, leaving you feeling insecure.

To make matters worse, a narcissist won't have an adult discussion when you confront them about their behavior. Instead of listening and trying to understand how you feel, they will roll their eyes and say you're overreacting. This is a form of gaslighting and is designed to make you feel crazy. You will start to wonder whether you are hypersensitive and unreasonable.

Research suggests that grandiose and vulnerable narcissists both deliberately make their partners jealous, but their motives are different.[26]

Grandiose narcissists are more strategic when it comes to jealousy, using it as a means of testing a relationship. For example, a grandiose narcissist may make their partner jealous by talking about an attractive co-worker. From the narcissist's perspective, if their partner stays with them despite being subjected to this kind of manipulation, the relationship must be strong or "real."

Vulnerable narcissists are more likely to act from a place of insecurity. They want to reassure themselves that their partner wants them. For example, they may seize the chance to flirt with someone else at a party so that their partner will get upset.

11. *They try to tell you how to live your life.*

If you dare to disagree with their assessment of a situation, they will start a fight or find another way to punish you. They take great delight in saying "I told you so!" at every opportunity.[27] They prefer to be right instead of being kind.

12. *You can never win an argument.*

Narcissists aren't interested in fair exchanges, and they don't want to reach compromises. They don't understand the concept of respectful disagreements.

13. *They cheat on you.*[28]

Not all cheaters are narcissists, and not all narcissists cheat. However, research has shown a link between the two. Given that there isn't enough attention in the world to satisfy a narcissist, this shouldn't come as a surprise. The more supply they have in their lives, the better they feel.

Note that "cheating" doesn't necessarily mean a full-blown sexual affair. Narcissists aren't always crazy about sex. Their priority is getting attention, so emotional affairs also appeal to them.

14. *They are performance-driven and distant in bed.*[29]

For some narcissists, sex is a chance to perform. They aren't interested in meaningful, loving sex. In fact, they aren't capable of such intimacy. If you suspect that they are more concerned with their sexual prowess than your enjoyment, you're probably right.

Narcissists may put pressure on their partner to have sex whenever they want it. They may even co-erce or assault their partner, showing no regard for their wellbeing. They don't bother to learn about their partner's fantasies and preferences. If you try to tell them what you'd like in bed, they might belittle you or imply that your desires are abnormal and deviant.

15. *They are violent or give the impression that they may one day hurt you.*

    Psychologists have found links between narcissism and domestic violence, antisocial behavior, sexual coercion, and sexual aggression. Narcissists are also inclined to accept these behaviors in other people.[30]

16. *Your other relationships are under strain.*

    Narcissists may cut their victims off from their family and friends. This lets them retain control over their partner and keeps them from talking to people who can point out the narcissist's flaws and abusive behaviors.

    A narcissist may try to undermine your friendships, family relationships, and even professional relationships. Instead of telling you that you are no longer allowed to meet with other people, which is obviously abusive, the narcissist might resort to more underhanded tactics.

    For example, they may claim that your friends are a bad influence on you, that your parents don't love you, or that your professional acquaintances are speaking badly of you behind your back. These tactics are designed to make you feel insecure, and therefore more dependent on the narcissist for approval.

The Narcissistic Love Script

The first time someone encounters a narcissist, they assume that their experience is unique. In reality, millions of people have suffered the same fate.

According to therapist Elinor Greenberg, who specializes in treating narcissistic behaviors, narcissists cycle through distinct phases in their relationships. She calls this process the "Narcissistic Love Script."

It goes like this:[31]

Phase 1: Courtship

The narcissist love-bombs their victim. They shower them with flattery and praise, making them feel like the most special man or woman on the planet. The narcissist might even talk about marriage after only a few weeks of dating.

In some cases, the narcissist knows that they are lying to their new partner, stringing them along in return for sex or an ego boost. But some narcissists really believe their own lies. They genuinely think that they've found someone who can make them happy and whole. Sadly, they aren't trying to know their partner as a person. Instead, they are merely treating them as a player in the narcissist's personal fantasy of finding "perfect love."

Phase 2: Persuasion

Inevitably, the narcissist has to confront reality. No one can live up to their impossible ideal of the perfect partner. Instead of moving on and finding someone who is a better fit or adjusting their expectations accordingly, the narcissist tries to change the other person.

They start to make what they think are helpful suggestions. Their aim is to mold their partner into their ideal fantasy figure. They might tell them to lose weight, dress differently, push harder in their career, find better friends, and so on.

At this point, the relationship turns abusive and unhealthy. The narcissist shows little empathy and acceptance. They are merely on a mission to refashion the other person to fit their own personal narrative.

Phase 3: Devaluation

If a narcissist's partner doesn't go along with their suggestions, they will be punished. Because they see the world in black-and-white terms, the narcissist sees everyone as either an ally or an enemy.[32]

Narcissists can't simultaneously love someone and acknowledge their anger or disappointment. They can flip from "positive" to "negative," and there is no setting in between. This is why a narcissist seems to have no inhibitions when it comes to starting fights or insulting their partners.

If you don't go along with what they want, they will knock you off the pedestal they put you on early in the relationship and begin to devalue you. This can take the form of insults, infidelity, gaslighting, and other forms of abuse. At this stage, you might cling on in the hope that the love bombing stage will come back. Unfortunately, once you have been devalued, you'll never receive such good treatment again.

Phase 4: Controlling Behavior

Having gotten into the habit of devaluing and insulting their partner, a narcissist will then feel confident in ramping up their controlling behavior. Because they no longer see their partner as someone to be revered and adored, they have no problem in treating them as an inhuman object. Domination gives the narcissist a sense of power.

A narcissist will look through a partner's texts and emails or spend hours scrolling through their posts on social media. They treat their partners like naughty children in need of guidance.

When a narcissistic partner treats you this way, your self-esteem will start to crumble. You'll feel increasingly dependent on them for validation and affection.

Phase 5: The Narcissistic Discard

Finally, the narcissist realizes that they will need to look elsewhere for the man or woman of their dreams. Of course, this mythical being does not exist, but it doesn't stop them fantasizing that they will someday find somebody perfect.

A narcissist might drop their partner with little prior warning, especially if someone else has grabbed their attention.

Some narcissists cycle through relationships quickly because they are easily bored. They may come into your life, speed you through a whirlwind romance, and then move on to the next person once they've "won" you.

Others will drag the cycle out for a lengthy period of time, sometimes even years. Nevertheless, they eventually become disappointed and start "checking out." The narcissist might tell you that they have no other choice but to leave because you are so fatally flawed.

Note that your narcissistic partner needs a source of narcissistic supply, so they might find and line up your replacement before discarding you. They will then repeat the whole cycle with their new love, who will be told, at length, why they are so much better than you.

Why Is It So Hard To Leave?

Most people who find themselves in a relationship with a narcissist know, on some level, that they need to leave. However, breaking up with a narcissist isn't easy. In the next chapter, we'll look at why it's difficult to walk away.

Summary

- Narcissists are often highly attractive, and they do a good job of convincing people that they are looking for a serious relationship.
- Narcissistic people see their partners as a source of approval and attention, rather than equals.

- Narcissists tend to follow roughly the same script every time they start a romantic relationship.
- If you stop offering them the narcissistic supply they crave, a narcissist will discard you.
- You can recognize that your relationship needs to end, yet still falter when it comes to actually packing your bags and leaving.

CHAPTER 8:

WHY DO PEOPLE STAY WITH NARCISSISTS?

To the bafflement of their family and friends, intelligent men and women stay with their narcissistic boyfriends, girlfriends, and spouses, sometimes for decades.

If you're in this kind of relationship yet can't seem to end it, there's nothing wrong with you. You aren't broken or masochistic. Once you understand the psychological principles involved, everything will start to make sense.

Note that this information applies to friendships and family relationships too. You don't have to be romantically involved with a narcissist to fall into these traps.

IT'S ALL TOO EASY TO REMEMBER THE GOOD TIMES

No one is 100% "good" or 100% "bad." Yes, your partner might be making your life extremely difficult, but they might still be fun, attentive, and generous at times. After all, you wouldn't have been sucked in if they hadn't been able to show these qualities. It's natural to hope that your partner will revert back to how they used to be.

> *Reality check:* The relationship will never be as enjoyable as it was in the early days. What's more, even if they did turn back into the person you once knew, how could you trust that they've reformed for good? It's easy to get stuck in a cycle whereby an abusive partner promises to change, acts nicely for a short period of time, then resumes their abusive behavior.

Take a close look at each stage of your relationship. Work out how much time you've spent feeling happy with your partner. For example, let's say you've been with your partner for three years, or 36 months.

Perhaps the first three months were fantastic, and you've had a couple of great months here and there over the past couple of years. Even assuming that you've enjoyed a total of 12 wonderful months together, that still means that your relationship hasn't been very good for 66% of the time. Is staying with this person really the way you want to spend your life?

THE SUNK COST FALLACY

If you've invested a lot of your time and effort into a relationship, you might fall victim to a thinking error known as the "sunk cost fallacy." All too often, people are reluctant to leave their partners because they think, "Well, I've come this far, it doesn't make sense to throw in the towel just yet."

The years go by, nothing changes, and it becomes increasingly harder to leave.

> *Reality check:* The past is gone, and you have to accept that you can't get that time back. All you can do is take stock of your relationship in the present and act accordingly. It makes no sense to waste yet more time on someone who can't be the empathetic, caring partner you deserve. By staying in an unhealthy situation, you are denying yourself the opportunity to find a better match.

THE "I CAN FIX IT" MENTALITY

Do you tend to assume that, with enough effort, you can overcome any challenges life throws your way? Determination is an admirable trait, but it can get you into trouble when you hang onto a partner who isn't doing you any favors.

You're more likely to fall into this trap if you are the nurturing type. For example, some caring women find it hard to leave narcissistic men because they believe that all their partners need is love and time.

> *Reality check:* Some things can't be fixed. Stepping away from a relationship that is making you unhappy isn't a sign of weakness. Narcissism is a firmly entrenched pattern of beliefs and behaviors that is hard to shift without professional intervention.

If you love helping others, try directing that impulse towards yourself. Have you been neglecting your health, hobbies, career, or friendships? It's not selfish to make yourself a priority in your own life. You can also channel your nurturing instinct into charity work.

POSITIVE & NEGATIVE REINFORCEMENT

If you are rewarded for a behavior, you are more likely to repeat it again in the future. This holds true for humans and other animals. Psychologists call this "reinforcement."

Positive reinforcement involves some kind of reward. For example, if you text your partner and they quickly respond with an uplifting, loving message, this is positive reinforcement. As a result, you are more likely to send them messages in the future. If a behavior isn't reinforced, it weakens and then dies out altogether. This is called "extinction."

Negative reinforcement involves the removal of something unpleasant. You learn that doing something will relieve some kind of pain or discomfort. For example, if you change your outfit before you go out with your partner because it's the only way to stop them complaining that you look bad, this is negative reinforcement. You will be more likely to give in to their demands in the future because you have learned that it will shut down their complaints.

Consciously or not, narcissists use these psychological principles to their advantage. By showering you with grand gestures and loving words in the early stages of your courtship, they are using positive reinforcement to get you to stick around. Later, they will use negative reinforcement to teach you how to placate them.

When you are caught up in the drama of an unhealthy relationship, it's hard to spot these patterns. Keeping a log of the highs and lows can help you unpick the dynamics between you and your partner. After a few weeks, or even within a few days, you'll start to notice how they keep you hooked.

WHY A RELATIONSHIP WITH A NARCISSIST IS LIKE A TRIP TO THE CASINO

The American psychologist B.F. Skinner, who demonstrated the basic principles of reinforcement in pigeons and rats, was also interested in the psychology of gambling. Specifically, he wondered why people are willing to spend lots of money on fruit machines and roulette wheels when they only have a relatively small chance of winning a prize.

He decided to investigate this phenomenon by changing the way he rewarded the animals in his experiments. The rate of rewards is known as a "schedule of reinforcement." For example, rewarding a rat with a food pellet every time it presses a lever is known as a "continuous schedule of reinforcement." Rewarding a rat at random is known as a "variable ratio reinforcement schedule."

Skinner discovered that if you give a rat a food pellet every time it presses a lever, but then stop after a few trials, the rat will quickly figure out that it won't get more pellets. It will stop pressing the lever because it understands that the supply has run out.

However, variable ratio reinforcement produces behavior that resembles addictive gambling. A rat might only get a reward occasionally, but it will nevertheless keep on pressing the lever in the hope of "winning." Rats on a variable ratio reinforcement schedule are like people who spend hours playing fruit machines, hoping that they will strike it lucky on the next turn.

What do gambling rats have to do with narcissistic relationships? Well, just as the rats only needed occasional reinforcement to keep pressing the lever, human beings will keep persevering in relationships that only reward them some of the time.

For example, let's say you are dating someone who was very attentive during the first few weeks of your courtship but has recently taken long to respond to your text messages. What's more, their replies have become shorter, and you get the feeling that they are no longer as interested in you. You feel anxious because you really like this person and had started to imagine a future together. (This is especially likely if the other person is a narcissist who lavished time and energy on you in the beginning, fooling you into thinking that the two of you had something really special.)

Let's say you've sent them two messages but haven't heard back. Now imagine that you send them yet another message, but this time you receive a long, gushing reply in which they apologize for neglecting you. Perhaps they even suggest going out to dinner that evening. You feel a mix of elation and relief. Your patience and messaging has paid off. You had to wait a long time, and send them lots of messages, but you finally got the outcome you wanted—positive attention and excitement.

Just like one of Skinner's rats, you've been conditioned. You are now in a pattern—you send messages, feel worried, but then enjoy a rush of happiness when you occasionally get a positive response. Your partner doesn't even need to treat you well most of the time to keep you invested in the relationship. Throwing you a few crumbs every so often is enough to ensure your loyalty.

No matter how rational and intelligent you are, you can quickly get locked into this pattern. If you've ever felt addicted to a toxic partner, you weren't far off the mark! It takes determination, time, and self-compassion to wean yourself from a narcissist.

TRAUMA BONDING

A "trauma bond" is a compulsion to remain in a relationship with someone who abuses you, even when you know that you need to leave. It's caused by a combination of intermittent reinforcement, together with the hormonal shifts you experience during the cycle of abuse.[33]

Abusers often behave badly, promise you they will change, pretend to care about you for a while, only to then repeat the process all over again.

During the times they act out and abuse you, your body releases cortisol, which is commonly known as the "stress hormone." High cortisol levels cause unpleasant side effects, including stomach problems, pains, and fatigue. In the long term, having too much cortisol circulating around your body will increase your risk of serious conditions, such as diabetes and heart disease.

However, when your partner offers to reconcile or behaves in a remorseful way that makes you feel relieved, your body releases dopamine. This chemical is often referred to as the "happy hormone," and makes you feel calm and reassured. The rollercoaster of emotions you feel in an abusive relationship becomes addictive. The longer this goes on, the stronger the trauma bond becomes, and the harder it is to walk away.

Breaking trauma bonds is painful. You may know that your ex is a toxic narcissist, yet you feel compelled to resume the relationship. It's like coming off drugs. You will need to stay vigilant after leaving your ex because they will know you are in a vulnerable state of mind and will try to draw you back into the relationship. They may promise to change, tell you that they are going to therapy, or that everyone deserves a second chance.

Another favorite tactic of abusers is to claim that they are in dire need of help. For example, they might claim that they are very depressed and will kill themselves if you don't help them. Or they might plead poverty or say they have nowhere to stay.

As harsh as it may seem, you need to realize that you aren't responsible for fixing anyone else, narcissist or not. It isn't wrong to put your peace of mind first. These dirty tactics aren't new. Narcissists have been practicing them forever. Don't fall for their lies.

SUMMARY

- Anyone can end up in a toxic relationship.
- Understanding a couple of psychological theories can help you understand why people stay.
- Intermittent reinforcement can fuel relationship addiction, leaving you eager for any crumb of affection or attention.
- Trauma bonds can make it hard to leave an abusive relationship, locking you into a cycle whereby you are eager to please your partner but cannot live up to their unrealistic or ever-changing standards.

CHAPTER 9:

BREAKING UP WITH A NARCISSIST

Ending a relationship with a narcissist is tough, but it can be done. In this chapter, we'll look at what you can do to make the breakup less painful.

HOW DO NARCISSISTS RESPOND TO A BREAKUP?

No two breakups are quite the same, but a narcissist will generally respond in one of two ways:

1. They will immediately cast you aside, cut all contact, and act like you never existed.

2. They will try everything in their power to get you back, possibly accompanied by smear campaigns against you if you don't agree to resume the relationship.

Both outcomes are painful. It hurts to be dismissed by someone who claims to have loved you. On the other hand, it's exhausting and sometimes frightening to be on the receiving end of a narcissist's rage.

Either way, don't expect an amicable separation. Narcissists take rejection as a grave insult, and they can hold a grudge for years.

DON'T EXPECT THEM TO UNDERSTAND

Narcissists rarely understand why their partners want to end a relationship. You can spend hours telling your ex why their behavior is hurtful, but they probably won't get it. Don't expect an apology, either, unless they think it will help them get back in your good books.

Even if they have a terrible track record of bad behavior, your ex may try to pin the blame on you. For example, if they cheated, they might say that you drove them into someone else's arms. If you end the relationship because they are pathologically jealous, they might claim that they are only possessive because they care so much.

BE PREPARED FOR EMPTY PROMISES

Remember, a narcissist can be a great actor. Because they are shameless and don't mind manipulating others to get what they want, you might be treated to dramatic fake apologies. It takes a lot of strength to stand firm and realize that they aren't trying to establish a better relationship. They just want to win you back so they can regain control of the situation.

Your ex may claim that they will change, that they know how much they've hurt you, and that they've never loved anyone else the way they love you. Although this sounds poetic and romantic, it doesn't mean anything.

"You'll Never Make It Without Me"

Your narcissistic partner assumes the world revolves around them. In their eyes, they are a great catch, so why on earth would you break up with them? They might even delude themselves into thinking that you can't survive in the world without their so-called help and support. Be prepared to hear things like "You won't get by on your own," and "It's thanks to me that you've gotten anywhere at all."

Convinced of their own superiority, your ex may even tell you that you'll never find anyone as good as them, or that no one else will ever love you. These are all lies. You can, if you wish, find a partner who is better and more loving in every way. A narcissist can erode your self-esteem, but you can rebuild your life with enough time and the right support.

Getting Away From An Abusive, Dangerous Narcissist

Not all narcissists are abusive, but narcissism and abuse often go together. If your narcissistic partner becomes abusive or threatening, call the police. Just having the call on record can be useful at a later date if you press charges for assault or harassment.

Living with an abusive narcissist is dangerous, but leaving them is even riskier. Three-quarters of women murdered by their abusive partners are killed when they try to end the relationship.[34]

You may need to leave quickly if the abuse escalates. Pack a bag containing a change of clothes, money, medications, and copies of your important personal documents. If you can tell a friend or relative about your situation, they will be prepared to spring into action if and when the need arises. If you have children, you'll also need to take copies of their passports and medical records.

Your local domestic violence shelter or women's charity can help you make a short or long-term exit plan. They will have experience in helping people get away from narcissistic partners. You can still reach out to a woman's charity if you are male; they will be able to put you in touch with people who can assist you.

Leaving a domestic abuser isn't easy. Victims often have to think about their financial situation, access to their children, and how they will cope emotionally with the loss of their relationship. There is no shame in asking for support. It could save your life.

KICKING A NARCISSIST OUT OF YOUR HOUSE

If your home is rented or mortgaged in your name only, and you are not married, you can ask your partner to leave. You have no moral obligation to wait until your ex has found alternative accommodation. Your safety comes first.

However, there's a good chance that they won't go quietly. You may need to involve local law enforcement or get a court order forcing them to stay away from you.

If you are married, it's not as simple as ordering them to get out, even if you are the sole owner of the property. Depending on your circumstances and where you live, they might have a right to remain in the marital home. You'll need to consult with a lawyer to discuss your options.

THE NO CONTACT RULE

Dr. Judith Orloff, who specializes in helping sensitive people navigate relationships, advises that it's best to go "cold turkey" when ending the relationship. Otherwise, your ex will continue to overstep your boundaries and manipulate you.

Cutting off contact will be very painful at first. Your relationship might have been your first priority for years, and getting rid of the narcissist will leave a void. It's normal to have a range of conflicting emotions. You might be relieved, sad, confused, and hopeful all at once. However you feel, it's the best way forward if you want to get rid of the narcissist for good.

Stop replying to their messages. Don't pick up the phone when they call. Block them on social media and change your email settings so that their emails go straight to your Trash folder. If you happen to see them in the street, discreetly change direction so you don't bump into each other.

If their friends or family members try to get in touch, do not engage. The moment you respond, you are encouraging them to keep trying. Remember, variable reinforcement is addictive! If you give them occasional feedback, they will keep trying to get a reaction from you.

There is one caveat to this rule. If they are abusive, don't delete their messages. You may need them later if you press charges.

No matter how many pent-up emotions you have inside, resist the urge to reach out and tell your ex how you feel. Vent to a trusted friend or therapist instead.

Think carefully before asking your ex to return any of your belongings. Unless it's something very valuable, it's best to write it off as a sunk cost. A narcissist with a grievance will make returning a few books, clothes, or other inexpensive items a pointlessly complicated and painful exercise.

LOW CONTACT

If you have children or work together, no contact isn't always a viable option. You will still need to keep one another updated on various matters. A low contact strategy is your best bet.

This takes a lot of patience and willpower because you might feel the urge to give them a piece of your mind. Don't! Before every interaction, separate what you want to say from what you actually need to tell them. Do not allow yourself to get dragged into arguments or drama.

If you feel a burst of destructive anger coming on, make an excuse to leave the room or conversation. Return only when your feelings are under control. When you talk to your ex, don't give them any insight into your personal life. Be civil and patient, but not warm or talkative.

Never assume that your narcissistic ex will reform. Get into the habit of documenting everything, even when things seem to be running smoothly. You never know when they will turn against you and start fabricating events and conversations that never happened.

Consider using an app to share and record important information. For example, the Our Family Wizard app lets you and your ex coordinate your child's schedule and manage expenses. The app also keeps a paper trail of messages, which can shut down any attempts to gaslight you.

DON'T GO IT ALONE

Even if your ex has never shown violent tendencies and seems happy to discard you, get some emotional support. If you don't already have a therapist, find one, preferably someone with a track record in helping people move on after abusive relationships.

In an ideal world, you'd be able to rely on family and friends for support, but this might not be possible for a host of reasons. For example, if your ex-partner has fooled everyone into thinking that they are the injured party, your family won't be sympathetic towards you.

WHEN A NARCISSIST COMES BACK

Narcissists have a habit of trying to get back into their exes' lives, sometimes years or even decades after the relationships have ended. Their return can throw you completely off guard. Why might someone suddenly get back in touch with you, when the relationship died so long ago?

The simplest explanation is that they are running low on narcissistic supply and think that you will be a good source of attention and approval. Even if you have moved on and are happy in a new relationship, they may still try to worm their way back into your life.

Don't let yourself get drawn in. Remind yourself of why you couldn't sustain a relationship with this person. Stick rigidly to the no contact rule. Trying to "be friends" or "just catch up" isn't a smart idea.

CHALLENGES OF DIVORCING A NARCISSIST

Getting rid of a narcissist is never easy, but things become even more complicated if you are married.

Here's why:[35]

1. *They play the victim.*

   A narcissist won't admit that they had any part in the breakdown of the marriage. They will tell everyone that you're the bad guy, and they are the wronged party.

2. *They will feel outraged that you have the courage to uproot their life.*

   A narcissist's friends and partner are there to prop up their ego and make their life easier. If you pull the rug from beneath their feet by filing for divorce, they will get angry.

3. *If you have children, a narcissist may use them as pawns in a divorce.*

   You'd hope that a narcissist would love their children enough to make your divorce as easy as possible. Unfortunately, they often use their children as weapons. For example, they might turn your children against you just to see you suffer.

4. *People may assume that you are both equally responsible for the breakup of the marriage.*
    Because your narcissistic ex is probably good at maintaining a façade, even those closest to you might ask painful questions about what you've done to drive your ex-spouse away.

5. *They don't play nice just because it's the right thing to do.*
    Some people believe in amicable divorce, but narcissists don't. They will try to suck up as much of your time, money, and energy as possible. They can hold onto a grudge for decades and may drag out the proceedings in an attempt to punish you.

HOW TO MAKE THE DIVORCE PROCESS AS PAINLESS AS POSSIBLE

1. *Hope for the best but assume the worst.*
    You may get lucky. Some narcissists, particularly if they've discarded their latest victim, aren't bothered by the prospect of divorce. Unfortunately, it's more likely that they will react badly and fight you.

2. *Get the best legal advice and representation you can afford.*
    Seek out a lawyer with experience in high-conflict divorce. It could be the best money you'll ever spend.

3. *Be prepared for your ex-spouse to do a 180 at any time.*
    They might begin by promising you an amicable

divorce but then turn on you once the reality of the situation sets in.

4. *Change your locks and passwords as soon as possible.*
   Don't trust your ex to respect your boundaries. Do all you can to keep them out of your home and online accounts.

5. *Look for support online from others who have been in your position.*
   A quick Google search will take you to blogs, articles, and forums created by and for people who have divorced narcissists and survived.

6. *Communicate with your ex-spouse only through your lawyer.*
   This helps you keep a safe distance and will deprive your ex-spouse of the attention they crave from you.

7. *Record everything.*
   Keep copies of all emails, texts, voice mails, and instant messages they send you. Record any instances of abuse and report them to the relevant authorities.

8. *Tell your side of the story, but don't assume everyone will accept it.*
   If mutual friends or relatives ask you about your divorce, feel free to tell them, but don't expect them to understand or believe you. Few people can understand what it's like to divorce a narcissist.

9. *Don't make snap decisions and try to stay calm.*

   Your narcissistic partner knows your weaknesses and is probably a master at triggering your emotions. Make a pact with yourself that when you feel angry or upset, you'll retreat from the situation as soon as possible and avoid making any major decisions.

10. *Stay consistent.*

    Do not give in to their demands for attention. If they harass you, ask your lawyer for help in filing a restraining order. Let your actions show your ex-spouse that they will face consequences for abusive behavior.

Summary

- If you break up with a narcissist, they probably won't disappear quietly.

- Don't waste your breath explaining why you are ending the relationship. They will not understand.

- No contact is the best way to go after you break up, but you might need to go "low contact" in some cases.

- Divorcing a narcissist is hard work, and you will need to find a lawyer and therapist with experience in handling high-conflict divorces.

- Don't expect everyone to believe your side of the story.

- Document everything, try to stay calm, and accept that your ex-partner is more concerned with "winning," not an amicable separation.

CHAPTER 10:

DEALING WITH NARCISSISTS IN THE WORKPLACE

A narcissistic co-worker or boss can make your job hell. In this chapter, you'll learn how to spot a narcissist at work, why they cause so much trouble, and how you can stop them from spoiling your day.

Here's how to identify them:[36,37]

1. *They are eager to take credit for your ideas.*

    Narcissists don't want to be part of a team. They want to be the star and will conveniently overlook everyone else's contributions. They will shamelessly steal your ideas. If you confront them, they'll deny it.

2. *They don't want to talk about their emotions.*

    It's not appropriate to share too much personal information at work, but narcissists are unusually reluctant to talk about their feelings.

3. *They enjoy occupying a leadership position.*

    If they aren't yet in a senior role, they believe it's only a matter of time before someone recognizes their brilliance. In extreme cases, they might believe that they are the only person who can save or lead the business.

4. *They quickly get angry or distant when you make a suggestion or offer some constructive criticism.*

    If you are their manager, a narcissist will still assume that they are more competent than you and will push back against even mild criticism. If they are your boss, they won't welcome any suggestions that contradict their opinions or ideas.

5. *They ingratiate themselves with anyone who can help them climb the company ladder.*

    Are you in a senior management position? Do you have valuable industry contacts? Don't be surprised if someone who seems to treat everyone else poorly tries to befriend you. Unfortunately, they aren't interested in striking up a genuine friendship. Beware!

6. *They dress better than everyone else in the office.*

    Some people like to spend a lot of time and money on their appearance. That doesn't necessarily mean they are a narcissist but be wary if they seem obsessed with how they look, or if they judge those who aren't so fashion conscious.

7. *They may appear to be listening, but they are just waiting for their chance to speak.*

    Workplace problems often come down to a lack of mutual understanding, coupled with poor communication. Narcissists aren't interested in anyone else's opinions but their own, and they seldom bother listening to their colleagues. Watch out for people who nod politely when you speak but seem glazed over.

8. *They use more swearwords than other people.*
   Research shows that narcissistic people tend to swear more than average and are more inclined to use sexual language and humor.[38] If you object to their crass jokes, they'll accuse you of being too sensitive.

9. *They are jealous of successful coworkers.*
   Narcissists view success as a zero-sum game. In their minds, someone else's triumph is a personal slight against them. They will try to put down high-performing coworkers, or even damage their reputation by spreading false rumors. On the flip side, a successful narcissist will assume that everyone else envies them.

10. *They exaggerate their professional accomplishments.*
    To make themselves look good, a narcissist will subtly or overtly draw attention to their qualifications or experience. They are happy to lie about their career path, their college major, or previous job titles.

11. *They assume that office or company policies don't apply to them.*
    Your narcissistic colleague may rack up inappropriate business expenses, take lunch whenever they

please, or decide that they won't attend a mandatory meeting because they "have more important things to do."

12. *They don't pitch in to help with menial or boring tasks.*[39] You won't find a narcissistic employee cleaning the mugs in the breakroom or offering to sort the recycling. They believe themselves to be above such trivial jobs.

HOW TO DEAL WITH A NARCISSISTIC COWORKER[40]

1. *Document everything.*
   Keep notes of all contributions you make to every project, ideally in digital form. Keep all emails and instant messages that show what you have done and when you did it. Now that more businesses are using workflow management software to assign and monitor tasks, this is easier than ever. If the narcissist tries to take credit for your ideas later, you'll have evidence to the contrary.

2. *Try to have important conversations in front of witnesses.*
   Sometimes, you can't have a conversation via email, and you have no choice but to discuss an issue face-to-face. Pick your timing carefully so that other people witness what is being said. They can back you up later if the narcissist tries to rewrite history. It's best to raise a topic during a meeting than behind closed doors if possible.

3. *Learn how to control your emotions.*
   Narcissists thrive on drama. Don't rise to the bait. Do whatever it takes to build emotional resilience. Try meditation, journaling, therapy, or working through your personal problems with a trusted friend. Take care of yourself outside of work, and you'll find it easier to cope with difficult colleagues.

4. *Make yourself seem uninteresting to the narcissist.*
   Don't share personal information or opinions on sensitive topics because a narcissist can and will use it against you later. If you can't avoid them, stick to neutral or professional topics of conversation. Limit your contact as much as possible.

5. *If you need help from a narcissist, open with a compliment.*
   In some cases, you will have no choice but to ask a narcissist for their help or cooperation, but you can turn the situation to your advantage. Appeal to their sense of superiority by opening with a compliment, then asking for their input. For instance, you might say something like, "You know so much about this, I'm sure you can help me. I need some expert advice on something."

6. *If you are interviewing candidates, watch for warning signs of narcissism.*
   It's tempting to hire someone just because they look good on paper and seem eager to work for your company, but don't overlook glaring red

flags. Be wary if a candidate speaks badly of their former employer, speaks at length about their accomplishments without being prompted to do so, or makes bold, unsubstantiated claims that don't quite add up.

7. *Don't take a narcissist's behavior personally.*
    Your working life will be easier if you remember that narcissists treat everyone like dirt. Sure, they can and do have favorites, but even those they seem to "love" will be on the receiving end of their vitriol at some point.

8. *Don't vent about a narcissist to your coworkers.*
    Keep your complaints to yourself. Narcissists are sneaky, and you never know who has fallen under their spell. There is a good chance that your remarks will find their way back to your narcissistic co-worker, and they will want to punish you for speaking out against them.

9. *If you have a narcissistic boss, ask yourself whether you can tolerate staying in a job that may not give you the chance to live up to your potential.*
    A narcissistic boss doesn't care about the wellbeing of their team members, and they feel threatened when a junior employee tries to rise through the ranks. Sometimes, they deliberately sabotage other people's efforts to get ahead.

    If you want to progress in your career, you'll need to make a tough choice. You can either stay in your current role and try to advance without making your boss feel threatened—which might be impossible—or you can look for a position elsewhere with a healthier work environment.

10. *If you need to pass on an idea or suggestion to a narcissist, emphasize how it would benefit them.*[41]

Your idea will be better received if it makes the narcissist's life easier, makes them look good, or both. Use "we" language rather than "I" to encourage them to take a collaborative view of a situation. For example, you could say, "This will make our lives easier because…" or "We all know you like to take a risk with new company policies, so maybe you'd appreciate this idea…"

11. *Give compliments when they behave well.*[42]

Some narcissists are always unreasonable, but others will occasionally show flashes of goodwill or politeness. If you can catch them in the act and give them some positive reinforcement, they may be inclined to repeat it in the future. For example, you could say something like, "I really appreciate you being so kind today," if they run an errand for you.

Don't expect miracles, but a little positive feedback never hurt anyone. Bear in mind that a narcissist might feign kindness to manipulate you later, so stay vigilant.

12. *If you supervise a narcissist, create a culture of transparency, teamwork, and accountability.*[43]

    Group settings make narcissistic behaviors more obvious. Everyone, even narcissists, is vulnerable to peer pressure when working as part of a team. They may think twice about speaking over other people if more assertive members of a team are willing to call them out on their unprofessional conduct.

Try to create an atmosphere in which people are happy to put forward their opinions, make mistakes, and learn from setbacks. By boosting everyone else's self-esteem, the narcissist will be less likely to get away with toxic behaviors.

Hold everyone to the same standards. Make sure your team knows what you expect of them and be ready to implement consequences where necessary. Narcissists need to learn that they will not be given leeway or special treatment.

Being consistent won't change their underlying feelings of entitlement, but it will make your life easier. You won't have to waste time and energy deciding what to do every time they flout the rules, and your team will thank you for being firm but fair. Otherwise, they will come to resent both the narcissist and you. The golden rule is to focus on your team first, not the narcissist. If someone comes to you with concerns, don't dismiss them. It's your responsibility to follow disciplinary procedures if a toxic employee is harming others.

MAKING A COMPLAINT ABOUT A NARCISSISTIC BOSS OR CO-WORKER

What should you do if you've tried the strategies in this chapter, but to no avail? What if you really love or need your job but can't stand the thought of another day working with a narcissist?

You could report your boss or co-worker, but it's not always the smartest move. In an ideal world, employees would be able to rely on their HR department to tackle narcissistic and bullying behavior at work.

Unfortunately, abusive people frequently get away with mistreating others in the workplace. HR staff may be reluctant to "rock the boat," especially if the narcissist holds a position of power or is in some way valuable to the company. You need to take a realistic look at your situation.

HR expert Liz Ryan advises trusting your gut instinct. If you suspect that you would be putting your job in jeopardy by making a complaint, you are probably correct.[44]

You need to be aware that filing a complaint could make the situation worse. If the narcissist finds out, they will set out to get their revenge. Because they are so manipulative, it's hard to tell who is and isn't under their spell. This is why it's so important to gather as much evidence as possible. E-mails, letters, instant messages, and notes from meetings can all strengthen your case.

If your other coworkers happen to mention that they have been having similar problems, filing a complaint together could be more effective than going it alone. If others have witnessed your narcissistic colleague's bad behavior, ask them whether they would be willing to make a statement. Testimony from a third party can give your complaint credibility, but you need to make sure you trust them not to collaborate with the narcissist.

Coach Marie McIntyre recommends emphasizing how your colleague's conduct is harming the organization as a whole when making a complaint. The sad fact is that most HR professionals and managers care more about the business than employee satisfaction. Turn this to your advantage by highlighting how your co-worker is harming your productivity, driving away customers, or creating an unpleasant atmosphere at work. Above all, stay calm and stick to the facts. Be realistic; it may be best to look for another position.[45]

SUMMARY

- Narcissists are all too common at work, and some manage to get themselves promoted to positions of authority.
- Narcissists take credit for other people's ideas, are reluctant to acknowledge their own feelings, and are hungry for power.
- You can defend yourself by learning to keep your reactions in check, recording all important conversations, and holding sensitive conversations in the presence of other people if possible.
- Do not gossip about a narcissist because they will react badly if they ever find out.

- Managing a narcissist is challenging because they think of themselves as superior to you.
- If a narcissist is making your working life a misery, be careful when deciding on your next move. In some cases, making a complaint to your manager or HR isn't worth the backlash.

CHAPTER 11:

HOW TO HANDLE A NARCISSISTIC FRIEND

A s the saying goes, "Friends are the family we choose for ourselves." For the sake of your mental health, you need to be picky about who you invite into your life. Your friendships should make you feel safe, supported, and accepted. A true narcissist can't be your friend in any meaningful sense of the word because they lack the capacity for empathy and reciprocation that make friendships so special.

In this chapter, you'll learn how narcissists usually behave in their friendships. We'll go through your options when it comes to dealing with a narcissistic friend.

READING THE SIGNS

So, what does a narcissistic friend look like?[46]

1. *They leave you feeling drained rather than inspired or happy.*

    No one can be cheery all the time but, as a rule, your friends should leave you feeling good about yourself and the world. If your friend is an energy vampire who likes to complain at length about their life and the world in general, watch out. They might be a covert narcissist who is using you as a source of narcissistic supply.

2. *They tell you how to deal with your personal problems.*
    Good friends offer a listening ear, without interrupting you, belittling your problems, or pushing their own agenda. A narcissist will give advice, whether or not you actually asked for it, then act offended if you don't do as they say.

3. *They gossip about your mutual friends.*
    Healthy, well-adjusted people don't put others down. Don't trust someone who takes delight in ripping someone else to shreds.

    Note that this isn't the same thing as expressing sincere concern about someone. For example, a friend that says something like, "I'm a bit worried that Sally's boyfriend is verbally abusive, what do you think?" isn't behaving badly. They are simply noting what they have observed and are asking for your opinion.

    On the other hand, if the same friend were to say, "Sally's so dumb, isn't she? She always picks such jerks!" then they are out of line.

    If they speak badly of other people who aren't around to defend themselves, how do you think they talk about you when you're apart? Don't kid yourself that you are the exception.

4. *They act as though they care and want to help, but then use your secrets against you.*

   True friends know how to keep a secret. They never abuse your trust. Under no circumstances will a true friend ever try to blackmail you by threatening to reveal embarrassing or incriminating information about you. Someone who does this never deserves a second chance.

5. *They have narcissistic friends.*[47]

   Research shows that narcissists like to hang out with other narcissists. If you've recently made a new friend but have seen a few red flags, ask to hang out with their regular social group. Watch how they behave with others and don't dismiss your gut feeling if it tells you that something isn't right.

6. *They can't fight fair.*

   Just like narcissistic parents and partners, narcissistic friends don't sort out differences in an amicable, respectful way. They prefer to browbeat other people or resort to manipulation to get their way.

7. *They expect too many favors.*

   Friends help each other out in times of need. In a healthy friendship, one person might be needier than the other at times, especially if they are going through a crisis. As long as it balances out over the long run, this is perfectly normal.

Unfortunately, a narcissist doesn't see friendship this way. They aren't interested in what they can do for you, only in what you can do for them. For instance, they may expect you to listen to their relationship problems on the phone every evening without bothering to ask whether you are in the mood to talk.

Narcissists keep score. If they ever give you a gift or do you a favor, they will expect to be paid back—with interest. Good friendships don't work like this, but a narcissist will always be counting what you owe them. If you upset them, they may use lines like "After everything I've done for you, you should be grateful!" or "I've been an amazing friend to you, and now you're throwing everything back in my face!"

8. *They are jealous when you spend time with other friends or when you start a romantic relationship.*
   Narcissists want and need to feel special. If they start thinking of you as their best friend, they will take it personally when you have the audacity to hang out with other people. In extreme cases, they might sabotage your relationships with other people. For example, your narcissistic friend might try to flirt or even sleep with anyone who shows an interest in you.

9. *They compare you to their other friends in a way that leaves you feeling inferior or excluded.*

A narcissistic friend may subtly or overtly put you down by rattling off a list of someone else's talents or accomplishments. The strange thing is, they are probably bragging about you to someone else! This kind of triangulation is a power move. It's designed to leave you wondering how the narcissist sees you. If you fall into this trap, you'll waste time trying to prove that you are just as good as their other friends.

10. *They don't celebrate your achievements.*

In fact, they appear jealous or unhappy when you enjoy success or a stroke of good luck. They might congratulate you, but then make snide remarks that belittle your accomplishments.

11. *You feel uncomfortable when introducing them to your other friends or partner.*

Do you have to give your other friends an in-depth briefing on this person's "quirks" or "difficult side" before you feel OK about making an introduction? It might be time to take a closer look at what is making you uneasy.

LETTING GO OF A TOXIC FRIENDSHIP

A narcissistic friend is unlikely to change. If they've been dragging you down for a while, it's safe to assume that they'll continue to make you miserable as long as you stick around. If you want something to change, you have two options:

1. Adjust your expectations, work on accepting your friend for who they are, and change how you behave around them.

2. Cut ties with them.

Neither option is easy. Let's look at each in turn.

Option #1: Adjust Your Expectations

The standard advice for anyone in a friendship with a narcissist is to run away and never look back. In most cases, this is the right thing to do. As a rule, narcissistic friends are more trouble than they are worth.

On the other hand, if you can set firm boundaries with your narcissistic friend, limit your contact, and enjoy their company only when it suits you, it may be possible to hold onto the relationship.

First, ask yourself this: Why are you friends with this person? Perhaps they are so extroverted that their confidence rubs off on you when you go out, and hanging out with them means you get to meet new people. Or you may have grown up together and cutting them out of your life would feel like cutting off your past.

Be honest. Once you have figured out what you have to gain by letting them stay in your life, you can work out how to enjoy the good stuff while distancing yourself from the darker side of their personality. You can draw up a list of rules around how and when you will see them, what you will do together, and what you will do if and when they cross your boundaries.

For example, let's say that you are holding onto a narcissistic friend because they are gifted at bringing people together and organizing events. Sometimes, you enjoy hanging out with them because they can be fun and charming. Unfortunately, they have betrayed you on several occasions by sharing sensitive information and have also tried to steal your past boyfriends.

In this case, you would need to work out how to hold onto the social aspect of the friendship whilst drawing up clear boundaries and consequences that protect you from getting hurt.

You may set the following boundaries:

- "I only socialize with this person in the presence of other people."
- "I only see this person once a month."
- "I don't share any information with this person that I wouldn't want others to know."
- "I never introduce this person to anyone I'm dating."

Warning!

This isn't an easy route to take. It requires a lot of self-awareness and a talent for assertive communication. Can you truly accept that your friend is, at best, an occasional source of entertainment rather than a close, supportive buddy? Can you accept that they will never provide you with a safe place to be yourself? Probably not. If you cling on to any hope you have that they will change, you are setting yourself up for disappointment.

Option #2: Cut ties with them.

This is easier said than done, especially if you've been friends for a long time, but resist falling victim to the sunk cost fallacy. Just because this person has been part of your life for many years doesn't mean they have earned a place in your future.

A slow fade could be the best option. Gradually reduce the time you spend with your friend. If they ask you why you haven't been in touch, tell them that you've been busy. Keep your excuses generic and uninteresting.

Unfortunately, if you have been very close to your friend, they will probably take offense when you distance yourself from them. Be prepared for a confrontation. They might try to make you feel guilty for "abandoning them." You will need to stand up for yourself and defend your boundaries.

In extreme cases, they might say or imply that you have driven them to the point of self-harm or depression. This is emotional abuse. You are not responsible for their actions or health. If you have reason to think they are genuinely at risk of self-harm or suicide, call an ambulance or one of their close relatives.

SUMMARY

- If you have a narcissistic friend, you probably already know in your gut that something isn't quite right.
- True friends lift you up, but narcissistic friends drag you down.
- It can be hard to let go of a friendship with a narcissist, even if they have treated you badly.
- You cannot change a narcissistic friend. You can adjust your expectations or end the friendship.
- A slow fade, rather than a dramatic confrontation, is usually the best route when cutting a narcissistic friend from your life.

CONCLUSION

Congratulations! You've now gained insight into the world of the narcissist. With this knowledge comes considerable power. You'll never fall under their spell again. From this moment on, you'll always spot the warning signs and protect yourself from their toxic behaviors.

If you have to live or work with a narcissist, you now have a set of powerful tools at your disposal that will make your life a whole lot easier and more enjoyable. If you have suffered at the hands of a narcissist early on in life, you'll be able to move on and embrace healthier relationships.

When you grow your self-esteem and defend your boundaries, narcissists will lose interest in you. You will find friends and partners who can offer the respect you deserve. If you have to deal with a narcissist at home or at work, your newfound confidence means you will no longer have to worry about walking on eggshells. You'll be equipped to deal with their bad moods, their rages, and their attempts at manipulation.

You'll also be able to support and understand victims of narcissistic abuse. Because you know precisely how narcissists keep people hooked, you'll be in a great position to support anyone who has been lured into a bad relationship.

Narcissism is a growing problem, but you can play your part in spreading awareness. By modeling positive relationships for other people, you are sending a clear message—unhealthy, toxic relationships are not normal.

If you suspect someone you know is affected by narcissistic abuse, why not point them in the direction of this book? The more people who understand narcissism, the better. By praising empathy and holding toxic people accountable for their actions, we can build a kinder society.

THANKS FOR READING!

I really hope you enjoyed this book and, most of all, got more value from it than you had to give.

It would mean a lot to me if you left an Amazon review—I will reply to all questions asked!

Simply find this book on Amazon, scroll to the reviews section, and click "Write a customer review".

Or Scan the QR Code on Your Phone:

Be sure to check out my email list, where I am constantly adding tons of value. The best way to currently get on the list is by visiting www.pristinepublish.com/empathbonus and entering your email.

Here I'll provide actionable information that aims to improve your enjoyment of life. I'll update you on my latest books, and I'll even send free e-books that I think you'll find useful.

Kindest regards,

ALSO BY
Judy Dyer

Grasp a better understanding of your gift and how you can embrace every part of it so that your life is enriched day by day.

Visit: www.pristinepublish.com/judy

Or Scan the QR Code on Your Phone:

REFERENCES

[1] WebMD. (n.d.). *What Is Narcissism?*

[2] Peisley, T. (2017). *Is narcissism common? The answer may surprise you.*

[3] Ibid.

[4] Ambardar, S., & Bienenfeld, D. (2018). *Narcissistic Personality Disorder.*

[5] Zajenkowski, M., & Szymaniak, K. (2019). Narcissism between facets and domains: The relationships between two types of narcissism and aspects of the Big Five. *Current Psychology.*

[6] Vaknin, S. (n.d.). *The Inverted Narcissist.*

[7] HealthDirect. (n.d.). *Causes of Narcissistic Personality Disorder (NPD).*

[8] Marissen, A.E., Brouwer, M.E., Hiemstra, A.M.F., Deen, M.L., & Ingmar, H.A.F. (2016). A masked negative self-esteem? Implicit and explicit self-esteem in patients with Narcissistic Personality Disorder. *Psychiatry Research.*

[9] Ronningstam, E. (2017). Intersect between self-esteem and emotion regulation in narcissistic personality disorder – implications for alliance building and treatment. *Borderline Personality Disorder and Emotion Dysregulation.*

[10] Ibid.

[11] Kaufman, S.B. (2011). *Do Narcissists Know They Are Narcissists?*

[12] Malkin, C. (2013). *Can Narcissists Change?*

[13] Wright, A. (n.d.). *How To Recover From Growing Up With A Narcissistic Parent.*

[14] Meyers, S. (2014). *Narcissistic Parents' Psychological Effect on Their Children.*

[15] McBride, K. (2011). *The Narcissistic Family Tree.*

[16] Hammond, C. (2018). *How To Heal From a Narcissistic Parent.*

[17] Esposito, L. (2018). *Learning to Parent Yourself as an Adult.*

[18] Hammond, C. (2019). *How to Set Adult Boundaries with Narcissistic Parents.*

[19] McBride, K. (2011). *Narcissistic Parents: Contact or Not?*

[20] Streep, P. (2016). *Toxic Mom? Going No Contact? 5 Things You Must Realize.*

21 Meyers, G. (2018). *How Do You Grieve the Death of a Narcissistic Mother?*

22 Adler, L. (2019). *5 Signs Your Kids Have a Narcissistic Grandmother.*

23 Gross, E.L. (2018). *Seven Signs You're Dating A Narcissist, According To A Clinical Psychologist.*

24 Ni, P. (2016). *8 Common Narcissist Lies.*

25 Brenner, G.H. (2017). *Do Narcissists Make Their Partners Jealous on Purpose?*

26 Ibid.

27 Greenberg, E. (2019). *How to Tell If Your Date Will Be a Narcissistic Mate.*

28 Ni, P. (2016). *8 Common Narcissist Lies.*

29 Ni, P. (2015). *8 Signs You're In A Relationship with a Sexual Narcissist.*

30 Blinkhorn, V., Lyons, M., & Almond, L. (2016). Drop the bad attitude! Narcissism predicts acceptance of violent behavior. *Personality and Individual Differences.*

31 Greenberg, E. (2017). *The Narcissistic Love Script.*

32 Neuharth, D. (2019). *14 Thought-Control Tactics Narcissists Use to Confuse and Dominate You.*

[33] Finlay, S.L. (2019). *Why trauma bonding makes it hard to leave abusive relationships.*

[34] Domestic Abuse Shelter. (n.d.). *Information on Domestic Violence.*

[35] Farzad, B.R. (n.d.). *How Does a Narcissist Handle Divorce and React?*

[36] Cain, A. (2016). *11 signs you're working with a narcissist.*

[37] Ni, P. (2015). *10 Signs Your Co-Worker/Colleague is a Narcissist.*

[38] Krauss Whitbourne, S. (2011). *A Day In The Life of a Narcissist.*

[39] Worthington, B. (2017). *The office narcissist: How to spot (and deal with) them.*

[40] Sarkis, S.A. (2017). *7 Ways to Cope With Narcissists at Work.*

[41] Brake, T. (2018). *15 Tips for Handling Narcissistic Colleagues.*

[42] Barker, E. (2017). *How To Win With A Narcissist: 5 Secrets Backed By Research.*

[43] Kets de Vries, M.F.R. (2017). *How to Manage a Narcissist.*

[44] *Ryan, L. (2017). Should I Report My Abusive Boss To HR – Or Is It Too Risky?*

[45] *McIntyre, M.G. (2017). Should You Complain About Your Boss?*

[46] Wong, B. (2018). *6 Glaring Signs Your Friend Is A Narcissist.*

[47] Gregoire, C. (2017). *This Is Why Narcissists Make Friends With Other Narcissists.*

Made in the USA
Columbia, SC
05 October 2024